So, You Want to Join
the Peace Corps...

So, You Want to Join the Peace Corps...

What to Know Before You Go

Dillon Banerjee

Ten Speed Press

BERKELEY   TORONTO

Ten Speed Press
PO Box 7123
Berkeley, California 94707
www.tenspeed.com

Distributed in Australia by Simon and Schuster Australia, in Canada by Ten Speed Press Canada, in New Zealand by Southern Publishers Group, in South Africa by Real Books, in Southeast Asia by Berkeley Books, and in the United Kingdom and Europe by Airlift Books.

Cover Design by Catherine Jacobes
Text Design by Poulson/Gluck

Library of Congress Cataloging-in-Publication Data
Banerjee, Dillon.
    So, you want to join the Peace Corps : what to know before you go /
    Dillon Banerjee.
    p. cm.
    Includes index.
    ISBN 1-58008-097-9 (pbk.)
      1. Peace Corps (U.S.)—Handbooks, manuals, etc. I. Title.

    HC60.5.B34 1999
    361.6—dc21
                                                        99-053048

First printing, 2000
Printed in Canada

1 2 3 4 5 6 7 8 9 10 — 03 02 01 00

CONTENTS

III. Peace Corps Training — Learning the Ropes

IV. Managing Your Money

V. Living Like the Locals

VI. Common Medical and Safety Concerns

VII. Staying in Touch with Home

VIII. The Social Scene

IX. The Toughest Job You'll Ever Love?

X. Rules to Live By — Peace Corps Policy

XI. Traveling Like a Pro

XII. Post–Peace Corps

Appendices

About the Author

Index

Acknowledgments

This book would not have been possible without the invaluable

input and guidance provided by my wonderful wife, Sarah,

who also served as a Peace Corps volunteer in Cameroon.

Others I wish to thank include Parin Shah, all of my returned

Peace Corps volunteer friends who contributed in various ways,

the Peace Corps for allowing me to use their statistics and policy

materials, and Holly Taines White, my editor at Ten Speed Press.

Peace Corps Acronyms

APCD .... Associate Peace Corps Director

CD .... Country Director

COS .... Close of Service

ECAM .... Europe/Central Asia/Mediterranean

ET .... Early Termination

HCN .... Host Country National

IA .... Inter-America

IST .... In-Service Training

NCE .... Noncompetitive Eligibility

NGO .... Nongovernmental Organization

PC .... Peace Corps

PCMO .... Peace Corps Medical Officer

PCT .... Peace Corps Trainee

PCV .... Peace Corps Volunteer

PCVL .... Peace Corps Volunteer Leader

RPCV .... Returned Peace Corps Volunteer

TOT .... Training of Trainers

Preface

This straightforward question-and-answer book is for anyone interested in becoming a Peace Corps volunteer. It sprung out of my own frustrations at being unable to find information on the "real" Peace Corps experience back when I was applying to be a volunteer. I remember trudging through the application process, filling out forms, and completing medical exams, all the while unsure of what, exactly, I was getting myself into. I knew as much about the Peace Corps as anyone else did—that it sends people overseas for two years to work and live in developing countries at the "grassroots" level. I had read through the information packets the Peace Corps sent me, but they were mostly promotional pamphlets and recruitment flyers which glossed over what, I knew, must be a more complex and comprehensive picture.

Thinking myself somewhat resourceful, I set out to find independent accounts of life as a Peace Corps volunteer in bookstores, career centers, and libraries. I wanted the real dirt on being lonely, getting sick, having enough money, dealing with hardships, accomplishing program goals, learning new languages, and so on. Surely someone must have returned from the Peace Corps eager to share their newly acquired knowledge with fresh recruits. Imagine my astonishment when I found nothing.

Undeterred, I barraged returned Peace Corps volunteers (RPCVs) with calls and e-mails. I contacted RPCVs who had served in places as diverse as Nepal and the Marshall Islands. The more people I spoke with, the more I came to understand two things: 1) this was the way most Peace Corps applicants gathered information to quell their curiosity, and 2) most Peace Corps applicants ask exactly the same questions. Fueled with that knowledge, I made it a mission to put this book together upon completion of my service overseas.

For two years I served as an agroforestry volunteer in a small village in Cameroon, West Africa. My life there was amazing and memorable in many ways yet, as I've come to find, most of my experiences were fairly typical for the Peace Corps. Life throughout the developing world shares a surprising number of commonalities when it comes to basics like health, safety, infrastructure, transportation, and so on. The Peace Corps world, too, can be surprisingly uniform when it comes to dealing with administration and policies, technical and language training, and program implementation. And life overseas as an expatriate entails challenging adjustments to culture, society, and environment that cannot be avoided. All of these areas and related experiences are detailed in this book, along with many more. I'm confident you'll find the information provided in the following pages helpful regardless of whether you end up teaching English in Mali or working with farmers in Guatemala.

Deciding to join the Peace Corps and live overseas for two years is not easy. The greatest hurdle is often a mental one: stepping into the unknown and hoping to find the strength, commitment, and flexibility to see it though. Not knowing what to expect raises the hurdle even higher. I hope the information here will put things into perspective and allow you to consider the Peace Corps in a less intimidating light. Regardless of what you decide, I hope you continue to pursue ways to help make this world a better one, all the while seeking adventure and fun in your life.

Happy Trails,

Dillon

Part I
Pre-Application Jitters

1
What is the application process like? How long does it take?

The application process can be arduous and seemingly endless. The Peace Corps receives over 120,000 inquiries each year from people interested in applying. Tens of thousands of those people submit applications, and only a fraction are eventually accepted. Beside the fact that the Peace Corps is a government agency, which, by definition, means it can be slow and bureaucratic, the sheer numbers of applicants combined with the excruciating detail each applicant must provide on the application make it easy to understand why the review process can last up to a year.

The Peace Corps tells potential recruits that three personality traits are invaluable during the application process: persistence, patience, and a sense of humor. Persistence is required because, without it, your application may sit unread on a recruiter's desk or in a Peace Corps in-box for months. Try as they may, the Peace Corps does not always review every application and forward every file in a timely manner. Every so often you'll need to prod and encourage them to keep the process moving. I knew an applicant who, after submitting his completed application, sat back and waited to hear from the Peace Corps. He never followed up with calls; he never thought to check on the status of his application. After almost six months of waiting, he received a letter notifying him that his application had been deemed "inactive." Apparently, having never heard from him, his recruiter assumed he had lost interest in joining.

Patience is a virtue for Peace Corps applicants simply because, even if you are persistent and hound the office with weekly calls, the entire process may take anywhere from four to twelve months. Why does it take so long? Because there are several steps one must take to navigate successfully through the system. They are, in a nutshell:

1. Filling out the application. This is no easy feat. The application is six pages long, and demands an account of every relevant course, internship, summer job, and hobby that may qualify you for one of the Peace Corps' programs. You must provide three references (two professional, one personal) and write two essays (detailing your

---

2

motivation to apply, and any past cross-cultural experiences) —
all in addition to the typical name, address, education level, and
social security–type questions. The OPM (Office of Personnel
Management) estimates that the Peace Corps application should
take approximately eight hours to complete. In reality, expect to
be filling in the blanks for a few days.

2. Once your application has been reviewed, the Peace Corps
determines whether or not you "fit" into any of their program areas.
If you do, you will be called into the nearest Peace Corps office for
an interview with a recruiter. The interview is a major screening
tool for the Peace Corps. It is their forum for evaluating your level
of commitment, maturity, and experience, and is your golden opportunity to sell yourself, your skills, and your ambition. During
the interview, expect to be grilled on your reasons for wanting to
join, your expectations, your hopes and fears, your strengths and
weaknesses, and your preferences with regard to the Peace Corps'
geographic and program areas. They may also ask you whether or
not you are dating anyone seriously—a red flag to help them identify volunteers who may quit before their two-year commitments
are fulfilled (see Questions 58 and 59 for more on early termination [ET]).

You should treat the interview as you would any other job interview. Be professional, confident, assertive, and prepared. Many
applicants assume that they can wear torn jeans and tie-dye shirts,
or show up without preparation since it's an interview for the Peace
Corps. Recruiters will be turned off by that. They are not looking
for applicants who come across as extremely liberal or laid-back;
they're looking for the best qualified applicants among thousands
of competitors.

3. Assuming the interview goes well, your recruiter will "nominate"
you for one of the Peace Corps' programs. Possibilities include education, health and nutrition, agriculture, forestry, small business
development, water and sanitation, and so on. For a complete listing
of Peace Corps programs, refer to Appendix C. If you aren't slotted
for a program that interests you, this would be the time to speak
with your recruiter about revisiting your qualifications as they may
relate to other programs.

You'll also be told the region of the world in which you will most likely serve, the language requirements for that region, and your approximate date of departure. On the one hand, receiving such information boosts your morale and provides exciting news for friends and family. On the other hand, once the initial impact wears off, impatience and frustration tend to grow. You'll quickly realize how much of the picture is still missing. You won't know the exact country assignment, the actual date of departure, the specific language(s) you'll be learning, or the details of the projects you will be working on. This is usually the stage that applicants find the most trying.

4. Step four is when you undergo a thorough medical and dental exam, while the Peace Corps checks on all of your references and validates the information provided on your application. All the while, your recruiter will be keeping his/her eyes peeled for specific openings that suit your qualifications. Timing is everything at this point. If your medical exam goes off without a hitch, hound the office to ensure that Peace Corps nurses review your file in a timely manner. Call your recruiter frequently to follow the progress of your background and reference check, and inquire about his/her efforts to place your name in an available and appropriate volunteer slot.

5. The last stage of the application process is receiving the coveted "invitation" for a specific program, in a specific country, leaving on a specific day. You will be invited, for example, to teach English as a second language in Niger, leaving August 3rd. You'll have only ten days to accept the invitation, so do some quick research and some serious soul-searching to be sure that you are committed and willing to go.

If you have doubts about the country to which you've been assigned—perhaps it's predominantly French-speaking, Muslim, and urban, whereas you had your hopes set on Spanish-speaking, animist, and rural—you may want to inquire about other possibilities. Be sure though that your doubts are substantial and reasonable, not impulsive or superficial, and communicate them clearly to your recruiter. If you bow out of your initial invitation because you've heard the food stinks and the beaches are dirty, you're likely not to receive another invitation down the line. If you feel your reasons are solid, however, consult your recruiter and ask about other possibilities in the near future which may be more in line with your desires and expectations. Stay flexible, and don't come across as demanding.

Throughout the application process, remember to maintain a sense of humor. As I mentioned above, you're battling a bureaucracy that is deluged annually with paperwork. They deserve kudos for managing to process as much as they do, but to an eager applicant whose life hinges on their decisions, each snag along the way can lead to a nervous breakdown. If you learn to laugh when you'd rather scream, you'll be more likely to emerge from the application process unscathed.

When you finally accept an invitation, you can breathe a huge sigh of relief and start spreading the word that you're going overseas to be a Peace Corps volunteer! You can begin reading up on your new country, contacting RPCVs who served there to ask them questions about their experiences, and preparing your belongings for a unique packing effort (refer to Question 11). You will have reached the end of a long and twisted road, and should enjoy it before the beginning of a much longer and more twisted road begins—the actual Peace Corps experience itself! Spend the intervening months between the invitation and departure doing all the things you need and want to do, knowing that it may be two years before you get the chance to do those things again. Say your goodbyes, see your favorite band, go to the latest movie, eat your favorite foods, visit good friends, and spend quality time with family. All the while, cherish the fact that you have been selected to embark on an adventure that few others have the privilege of experiencing in their lifetimes, and know that you are about to discover new things about the world, about others, and about yourself.

2 Am I qualified to join the Peace Corps?

The Peace Corps is asked this question frequently, and as a result has published a "program requirements" pamphlet, as well as a one-pager outlining various ways candidates can make themselves more competitive. Rather than repeat or paraphrase the information here, I've included both publications as appendices in this book, so flip back to Appendices C and D for the Peace Corps' official response to this question.

In addition to specific program requirements, be aware of a few core requirements all applicants must meet before joining the Peace Corps. Volunteers must, for example, be U.S. citizens at least eighteen years old and in good health (there is no upper age limit). Most PCVs (ninety-five percent) have bachelor's degrees, and several have advanced degrees and/or related prior work experience. Married couples with dependent children are not accepted into the Peace Corps; those without dependents may be accepted if both qualify for volunteer assignments (refer to Question 3). All applicants must undergo a comprehensive medical and dental evaluation certifying that they are capable of handling the physical and emotional rigors of Peace Corps service.

When completing the application forms, be sure to include every bit of related experience that comes to mind. Oftentimes applicants don't realize how important it is to be absolutely and completely thorough. If you spent a summer helping your mom with gardening in the backyard, you may qualify for the Peace Corps' agriculture or forestry program. If you took a CPR course as part of your Boy Scout merit badge, you may be selected for the health education program. If you took two years of high school Spanish, volunteered for a few days at a food shelter, or organized a backcountry camping expedition with your friends, include it on your application. Roughly fifty percent of PCVs hold liberal arts degrees, which means their technical experience often comes from extracurricular activities, summer jobs, or personal hobbies. No matter how trivial or inane some of your previous experiences may seem to you, if it sounds even remotely related to a Peace Corps program, jot it down.

3 What if I'm married and we both want to join?

Go for it! Peace Corps statistics show that seven percent of all volunteers are married (see Appendix A). There were a few married Peace Corps volunteers in Cameroon during my time there. One was a recently retired couple, the other was newlywed and had decided to join the Peace Corps early in their marriage (before having kids, mortgages, and all that good stuff). From my observations, both couples had a good experience and were glad they joined. If you are married and considering the Peace Corps, though, you should be aware of a few things.

First, the application process can be much longer for married couples. The Peace Corps places volunteers by matching program needs, as determined by requests from host country governments, with the skills of its applicants. Placing two people in the same country simultaneously requires requests from a country for volunteers under both programs for which the two qualify. In other words, if you are nominated to be an agroforestry volunteer and your spouse is slated for the health program, you must wait until a country has openings for both and hope that you can fill those spots simultaneously. There may also be complications if the training schedules for your programs are not synchronized. It may be that agroforestry in-country training starts in June, while health training doesn't start until September. These are just some of the kinks married couples face that may take the Peace Corps some time to iron out.

The Peace Corps will also want you to be aware that, if you are married, you may be tempted to lean more on your spouse than other volunteers or villagers for support, guidance, and companionship. Although, to a degree, this is natural and expected, if taken to an extreme it can result in couples feeling isolated from peers, counterparts, neighbors, and friends. Don't be discouraged, however, as there are numerous married couples in the Peace Corps who serve successfully and rewardingly. My advice is to contact the Peace Corps or send out inquiries on the Internet to communicate with returned volunteers who served with their spouses, and ask them about their experiences.

4 Can I serve in the Peace Corps with my boyfriend or girlfriend?

No. The only way to enter the Peace Corps with a partner and be posted in the same village is to be married. Otherwise, there are no guarantees that the two of you will even end up on the same continent. In fact, if you are involved in a serious relationship, be aware that the Peace Corps will inquire about the nature of that relationship during the application process. If they perceive your emotional attachment to be substantial, it will count as a strike against you. This is because a significant number of people who "early terminate" (ET) do so as a direct result of feeling homesick for their boyfriends or girlfriends. Many people get so wrapped up in the adventurous and romantic notion of becoming a Peace Corps volunteer in a foreign country, that they underestimate the feelings of isolation, loneliness, and insecurity which arise from time to time during the experience—feelings which may be compounded if the volunteer has left someone special back home. Most volunteers I know who left a boyfriend or girlfriend behind to join the Peace Corps were not in those relationships two years down the road. Distance and time are two skilled assassins of even the strongest bonds, and in the Peace Corps, those assassins are armed and dangerous.

5 What will my Peace Corps experience be like if I'm an "older" volunteer?

Approximately seven percent of Peace Corps volunteers are over the age of fifty (see Appendix A). I served with several older volunteers in Cameroon, and they absolutely loved it. In fact, in many ways, they seemed to have an easier time with the adjustments and hurdles that their younger colleagues often stumbled through. They were more directed, more assured of their reasons for being overseas, more open to meeting new people and experiencing new hardships, and more comfortable with relinquishing the luxuries of life in the States. Often, they had thought about joining the Peace Corps for years beforehand, so when they finally did it was the culmination of a long and thought-out decision process. In addition, older PCVs in many countries enjoy an inherent level of respect and authority from colleagues, program administrators, and host country nationals (HCNs) in general, simply because of their age. This "automatic" respect, which younger volunteers spend months (if not years) earning, greatly facilitates their adjustment to life and work overseas.

If you are an older applicant and have concerns about joining, the best thing to do is call the Peace Corps and speak with a recruiter. They can tell you the most common age-related issues regarding Peace Corps service, and put you in touch with older RPCVs who would be happy to discuss their experiences with you. You will have to undergo a more thorough medical examination, and tying up loose ends stateside before leaving may be more involved, but aside from that the application process will be no different.

One issue that older volunteers are often forewarned about is the "surrogate parent" syndrome they may face during training and, to a limited extent, during their entire two years. Moving overseas can be an unnerving ordeal, often transforming stolid college graduates into timorous youths. When this happens, whom do the youths reflexively turn to for solace and comfort? The person who most reminds them of mom or dad. If the older volunteer isn't careful, he or she may end up playing parent for thirty angst-ridden Gen Xers, depriving him/herself of an otherwise culturally enriching and personally rewarding transition into life in the developing world.

Older volunteers may also initially feel uncomfortable with the fact that the bulk of their support group is much younger than they are. They may feel out of place during Peace Corps parties, which are typically hosted by younger volunteers and more closely resemble college parties than placid social gatherings. Over time, however, everyone (young and old) finds their niche and settles into a pace of life and social interaction that they feel comfortable with. The older PCVs in my program ended up forging close and lasting friendships with people half their age, finding common ground in shared experiences and mutual support.

6 What will my Peace Corps experience be like if I'm gay?

Gay volunteers can generally expect to find support from Peace Corps administration and fellow PCVs. In some countries, organized support groups exist for gay and lesbian volunteers; in others it's less formal, but you can usually find support if you need or want it. The topic is covered in diversity sessions during training, and the environment within the Peace Corps community is often open and accepting. Which isn't to say every volunteer in the Peace Corps is open-minded about homosexuality. The volunteer community is, in some ways, a microcosm of society in the States and therefore includes its share of homophobes and the religious right. For the most part, though, expect an understanding and judgment-free environment.

The same cannot be said, however, for life in the village. In many parts of the developing world, homosexuality is either unrecognized (considered not to exist) or is thought of as abnormal and even insane behavior. Gay volunteers often have to gauge the social climate of their posts and decide on an individual basis whether they feel comfortable telling local friends and neighbors about themselves. Many gay volunteers feel pressure at their posts to act heterosexual in social situations, knowing that to do otherwise could have serious repercussions on their work and social lives. There are instances where volunteers meet gay members of the local community and date them, but rarely are those relationships made public. So be forewarned: as oppressive as society may seem in the States for homosexuals, it's even worse in most other parts of the world. There will, however, be support available to you from the Peace Corps administration and other volunteers, and it needn't prevent you from having a successful and fulfilling two years overseas.

7 What will my Peace Corps experience be like if I'm a minority?

The most trying aspect of the Peace Corps experience for minority volunteers is dealing with international stereotypes. Oftentimes these stereotypes are a direct product of imported videos, movies, slogans, and commercial products. Asian Americans may face constant jeers and jests by village kids who mimic the karate kicks of Bruce Lee while shouting "hee-yah, hee-yah" at full volume. African Americans may have to patiently explain, time and time again, that they are not as rich as Janet Jackson, or as dangerous as Mike Tyson.

Other frustrations faced by minority volunteers include constant challenges by host country nationals who refuse to believe that the volunteer is American if they are not tall, white, blonde, and blue-eyed. Surprisingly, the converse can also be a source of frustration. If an African American volunteer is sent to Africa, he may be surprised to find villagers referring to him as "white man," and treating him with the aloofness or indifference often afforded to white foreigners.

Incredible as it may seem, another source of frustration for minority volunteers may come from the Peace Corps volunteer community itself. Sadly, the Peace Corps microcosm may initially polarize, with nonminority PCVs gravitating toward a social and support network separate from that of minority PCVs. Although, over time, such lines inevitably blur, those initial instances in which minority volunteers feel alienated from both the HCN and general PCV community may prove overwhelming.

The Peace Corps addresses minority volunteer issues during in-country training diversity sessions. Second-year volunteers visit the training site and give talks, put on skits, and hold discussion groups about life in the Peace Corps as it pertains to minority and racial issues. You will also be able to talk to your program director and Peace Corps volunteer leader (PCVL) if you are encountering any unpleasant situations at post. Your fellow volunteers will be great sounding boards for venting frustrations, too. In all, the topic is valid and important, but not one which should prevent you from joining the Peace Corps.

8 Will the two years go by quickly or slowly?

Time is a roller coaster in the Peace Corps. You'll lose track of hours, days, even weeks at some points. Other times will go so slowly you'll think you're in the *Twilight Zone*. When work is plentiful and you feel adjusted to village life, days will pass in the blink of an eye. When you hit a lull or endure those inevitable periods of acute homesickness, the spaces between seconds will seem miles wide. On the whole, however, most returned volunteers will tell you that their time spent in the Peace Corps was the fastest two years of their lives.

You'll hear a common theory that your second year goes by much more quickly than your first. To a degree I think it's true. Your first year starts off with a bang, deceiving you into thinking that the entire two years will fly by regardless of what older, more experienced volunteers say. Everything feels new and exciting, adventurous and challenging. A few months into it, however, as the novelty begins to wear and the reality of your commitment begins to set in, you realize just how much time you have ahead of you. You'll peer into the tunnel convinced that there is no light at the end. The months from the middle to the end of your first year can be painfully slow.

As you commence your second year, however, you'll feel a growing sense of accomplishment and begin to realize how far you've come since swearing-in. As you take in the breadth of your successes—with regards to work, life, language, friendships, health, and so on—you'll also gain a new vantage point. You will have passed the "hump" (the halfway mark), making your remaining time in the Peace Corps seem to glide by much more smoothly.

To a large extent, the pace of your overseas experience will also depend on your attitude, outlook, and approach. Regardless of where on the curve you stand, the more aware of time you are, the slower it will pass. The more idle and bored you are, the slower it will pass. The more isolated, lonely, and anxious you feel, the slower it will pass. So have fun, realize you're doing something great and finite, be creative with your free time, and strive to get the most out of each passing moment.

9 Will I be lonely?

Yes. At certain points during your service, as you would during any other two-year period of your life regardless of where you were or what you were doing, you will feel lonely. Perhaps the greater question is, "Will I be lonely a lot?" or "Will I get so lonely that it will be unbearable?" Admittedly it really depends on you, your outlook, your personality, and your circumstances. But in most cases, the answer is no.

As a Peace Corps volunteer, certain experiences and concurrent emotions are amplified; the highs are really high, and the lows can be really low. When it's all said and done, however, you'll realize a nice balance was struck during your two years abroad which incorporated some of the most memorable moments of your life—good and bad.

For example, when you find yourself alone at post and you pop in a tape that brings back memories of home, or you get a letter from friends sharing experiences without you, the ensuing depression may, at times, seem extreme. Amid all the other hardships you'll face daily, even a pebble of loneliness can sometimes cause an avalanche of anxiety. On the other hand, an occasional wallow in the "lows" affords you the perspective of rejoicing in the "highs." Ironically it's those acute moments of loneliness or feelings of isolation that make the "Peace Corps moments"—those times when you realize you'd rather be nowhere else on earth—so great.

Loneliness is part of the Peace Corps package—part of what makes the experience both meaningful and rewarding when you come out the other end after two years. If you stick through the lonely points, you will experience life in a completely unique and meaningful way. Even if you don't learn squat about the things the Peace Corps wants you to learn, you'll learn a lot about yourself.

As clichéd as this may sound, there is something else that warrants mentioning here: there is a difference between feeling lonely and being alone. The longer you serve in the Peace Corps, the more you come to appreciate that difference. Initially you'll link the two together, feeling lonely most intensely when you are alone. But soon you'll begin to value your independence and understand that it provides you the opportunity and freedom to enjoy moments that the hectic pace of life in the States denies you. As you become integrated into your village or town, as you make friends with volunteers and host country nationals, as you get comfortable with your work and your new environment, you begin to covet those quiet, deeply personal times alone—times to reflect, to think, to relax, to read, to listen to music, to cook, to write, to sleep. When you get back to the States after it's all over, you'll realize the calming effect that time alone had on your spirit, and it will feel good.

10 What will I miss the most?

You'll get some interesting answers to this question depending on who you ask. Rather than try to tell you what I think you'll miss the most based on my experiences, I polled some of my RPCV friends and lumped their responses together in the list below. I figure this way you'll have a more comprehensive and entertaining picture of the possibilities. Here's what the group came up with, in no particular order:

> Pizza, movies, live music, microbrewed beer, skiing, donuts, cable TV, driving, happy hour, chips and salsa, snow, cereal, hot showers, Taco Bell, friends and family, flush toilets, roomy cars, Twizzlers, Sunday papers, jogging, orange juice, thick mattresses, margaritas, climate control, milk, chewing tobacco, mosquito-free evenings, good water pressure, potable tap water, Hershey's chocolate, real ketchup, privacy, 7-11s (or equivalent), telephones, Diet Coke, *Rolling Stone* magazine, *The Simpsons*, paved roads, packaged foods, Frosted Flakes, cold beer, pool tables, Ben & Jerry's chocolate chip cookie dough ice cream, frozen food, anonymity, Tower Records, carpeting, coffee shops, bookstores, customer service, e-mail, deli sandwiches, good batteries, the U.S. Postal Service, and fine wines.

The list goes on, but I think you get the idea.

Part II
How to Pack for
a Two-Year Trip

11 What should I bring?

I could probably write a whole book on this question alone. The thought of packing only eighty pounds worth of stuff to last you for two years is almost incomprehensible. How is anyone supposed to fit clothing, toiletries, cameras, tapes, books, toys, pictures, mementos, camping gear, shoes, journals, and so on into two bags and a fanny pack? And how does one even begin to calculate which items are necessities and which can be left behind?

Packing for the Peace Corps is not as difficult as it seems, but it can be if you're unprepared. Once you find out which country you are going to, you can start researching and making comprehensive lists. You can send out requests for packing suggestions on Peace Corps Web sites and chatlines through the Internet. You can scan through the Peace Corps' recommended packing list included in the Country Profile packet mailed to you (though take it with a grain of salt, as the lists are often outdated). You can call RPCVs who served in the country you'll be in, and pick their brains for hints on what to pack. You'll find that if you use common sense and gather as much information as you can, you'll be packed up and ready quicker than you'd think.

Without going into great detail about specific items to bring, I can provide some general guidelines that I think will prove useful for anyone anxious about packing for the Peace Corps. First, pack light. You will be moving to a different country, culture, and environment—not a different planet. There will be plenty of basic supplies available at local markets, stalls, and shops no matter where you are. Count on finding towels, soap, combs, toilet paper, disposable razors, sheets, pillows, blankets, pots, pans, silverware, various spices, film, batteries, pencils, envelopes, and other staple products locally. In other words, don't stock up on those items—you'll be wasting valuable packing space.

Also, people all over the world wear clothes. There are no Peace Corps villages I know of where the inhabitants literally run around naked twenty-four hours a day. This means clothes are available locally—some pret-a-porter, others made to order. In most developing countries, beautifully patterned cloth and basic textiles of all kinds are available in the markets, and the skills of local tailors often surpass their higher paid counterparts in the States.

What you may want to bring in the way of clothing are articles that can't be made or purchased easily overseas—items such as GORE-TEX rain gear; strong, durable hiking boots, shoes, and sandals; durable jeans; Thorlo-type socks; a warm wool sweater or fleece; good cotton bras and underwear; quality T-shirts; etc. You'll also want to pack a set or two of nice clothes (especially true for education volunteers). Many people in developing countries place a high value on appearance and will appreciate it if you dress well. What you bring should also reflect the variations of climate within your country, both seasonally and geographically. In Cameroon, for instance, dry season nights were much cooler and crisper than rainy season nights. Rainy season days were much more moderate than dry season days. And the Northwest and Adamoua provinces were much more mountainous and temperate than the rest of the country. Knowing this before I left the States helped me decide to pack a few warm clothes. Also, I discovered that the summit of Mount Cameroon, at around 13,000 feet, frequently dips below freezing. Since I planned on trekking up at some point during my two years, I packed gear that I knew would keep me cozy for that trip.

Aside from clothing, what else should you pack? Most basic toiletries, like I said earlier, will be available locally. You may, however, want to bring a favorite brand of shampoo, conditioner, soap, shaving cream, hair spray, deodorant, or other products that aren't available abroad. It's best to consult an RPCV from the area to find out exactly which toiletries should make it into your bags.

Many people wonder about film and batteries. I have found in all of my travels that film and batteries are prevalent, especially in bigger towns and cities. The question is, will they be so expensive or so low-grade that you should pack your own two-year supply? In my opinion, you should pack a good cache of Kodak and Duracell goodies, but don't try to stock up for the whole two years. If you have enough to last you a few months, it will suffice until you either find a place that sells them locally, or have someone from the States replenish your supply with a care package.

Regardless of whether you like to camp or not, I highly recommend packing a sleeping bag and sleeping pad. You'll find they come in handy when you're visiting other volunteers, when you're traveling to faraway places, and when you have guests come to visit. If you are an avid camper and you plan on any serious expeditions, bring a camping stove (an "international" model that can run off of multiple fuel sources), a water purifier, and anything else you'd pack for a backcountry trip in the States. Normally, camping equipment is made to be light and portable, so you'll be able to fit all your camping toys into your bags without sacrificing too much space or weight.

You should definitely bring a book or two of U.S. stamps. As I mention in Question 42, you will have plenty of opportunities to hand letters and small packages off to people who are returning to the States. Doing this not only significantly reduces delivery time, but also virtually guarantees that your mail will reach its destination. If, however, your mail is not stamped, you end up inconveniencing the deliverer and risking delay. Stamps weigh virtually nothing and take up practically no space. Just make sure they are the self-adhesive kind, not the ones you have to lick, which gum up in humid climates and end up sticking to each other long before you need them. Stamps are also easily mailed to you in a care package once you run out.

Another item that I would highly recommend bringing is a portable radio/cassette player with an external speaker, or a Walkman with speakers that plug into the headphone jack. During training you'll mostly use a Walkman as you walk to and from the training center, or when you hang out in your room at your home-stay family's house writing letters. As soon as you get set up in your village, however, you'll want to play your music while you're cooking, reading, socializing, or just zoning in your house. Walkmans with headphones, at that point, simply aren't practical.

Although you can probably pick up a little boom box or a generic type of Walkman and speakers in the capital of your host country, you'd do much better to buy one here and bring it with you. Electronics sold in most developing countries are imported or manufactured locally, meaning they are either exorbitantly priced or of poor quality. You'll find plenty of imitation brands and pirated labels (like "Sunny" radios and "Sonya" tape players), which may or may not last a month before catching fire or burning out. You'll find real Sony and Sanyo stereos for sale in glitzy electronics shops in the capital, but their price will include import taxes, levies, bribes, and a hefty profit margin—even after you've bargained till you're blue.

My advice is to pick up a good quality, basic, portable, reasonably priced radio/cassette player with speakers here and bring it with you. Just make sure it doesn't take up half of your packing space or weigh fifty pounds. If you anticipate having electricity at post, you may want to buy a transformer and converter set before you go—those items are also pricey and less dependable when purchased overseas. When you complete your service (COS) two years later, you can either sell everything to another volunteer, sell it to someone in-country, give it away as a gift, or bring it back with you.

Spices are often cited by volunteers as something they wish they'd brought more of. There are lots of basic spices available everywhere (salt, pepper, garlic, ginger, hot peppers, etc.), but if you have some favorites and aren't sure if they are sold overseas, bring your own supply. Better yet, bring the seeds—you'll have the time and means once you are set up in your village to start a garden or spice patch. After all, the only thing better than good spices are fresh, organically grown, handpicked good spices.

Lastly, keep in mind that your country of service will be your home for two years, so save room for items that may not be "necessities" in the traditional sense of the word, but that you wouldn't want to go two years without. This includes pictures, favorite posters, objects of sentimental value, your favorite stuffed animal, and whatever else reminds you of home or makes you feel secure. If some of these items won't fit in your baggage, don't fret. Remember that you can have items sent to you (especially smaller, less critical ones), and pack accordingly.

12 Can I really only pack eighty pounds to take with me?

Yes and no. It's a good idea to stay around the eighty-pound mark, but I've found (especially in talking with other PCVs) that it's not exactly a "hard" target. Peace Corps wants to prevent you from packing everything you own in a panicked effort not to forget anything. If that limit didn't exist, people would walk into the airport with suitcases stuffed with everything from kitchen appliances to gym equipment. Although the weight limit may seem a bit low for a two-year life experience, it keeps you from overdoing it and forces you to prioritize.

That said, I was shocked to see trainees in my group lugging piles of baggage that clearly surpassed the allotted limit by a good twenty or thirty pounds. I was even more surprised to see those bags tagged and loaded onto the plane right alongside my sparse and trim lot, with no penalty or consequence. I was later told that Peace Corps is granted a predetermined "group weight limit" on their flights which they must not surpass. In other words, as long as some volunteers come in underweight, others can pack overweight loads.

Keeping this in mind, don't fret if you weigh your bags and discover that, with all the paring and trimming, you still come out a little heavy—especially if you've determined that there are no more items you may be able to do without. Odds are no one will notice or care, and a few of your fellow trainees will make up the difference by packing light and, by default, tossing a few extra pounds of allotment your way.

13 What kinds of games and toys should I bring?

You should bring games you can play by yourself, games that you can easily teach others to play, and small, challenging games that won't bore you easily. For example: cards, Scrabble, Yahtzee, cribbage, a hackeysack, a computerized chess board, backgammon, dominoes, a Game Boy, and so on. Games are treasured in the Peace Corps, especially in countries where volunteers don't have televisions or movie theaters to rely on for entertainment. Reading can get old and doesn't quite cut it as a social event when you have friends over. Eating, drinking, and conversing are always fun, but when you hit the inevitable lull, games can spice things up.

Besides bringing games for your own entertainment, they serve as excellent ice-breakers and kid-pleasers at post. I had some of my greatest laughs in the village teaching Cameroonians how to play American card games, and hackeysacking with my neighbors. And when you leave the Peace Corps, all those trinkets and game boards make perfect gifts.

14 How many books and tapes should I bring?

Books and tapes are the movies and videos of the Peace Corps. They are the primary form of escape, entertainment, diversion, distraction, relaxation, and therapy for volunteers worldwide. Never in your life will you have such a devoted opportunity to read as many books as you can and want, to enrich your mind and broaden your thoughts. You will come to view your tapes and music as doors to other places, people, and times. And the beauty of it all is that everything is already over there, for the most part.

Volunteers come and go like the wind, and most of them like to pack light. This means that entire libraries of books and tapes collect in Peace Corps offices, rest houses, volunteer's shelves, and training centers. And the supply is continuously refreshed by new volunteers, care packages, tourists, and visiting family and friends. So don't worry too much about hauling books and tapes with you when you leave the States.

You should, however, carefully select the music that you absolutely can't live without, and pack some blank tapes to copy music onto once you get over there. Similarly, you should choose a handful of books that you've been dying to read, especially newer ones that may not yet be circulating. Then get ready to plug into an amazing network of low-tech entertainment, and enjoy.

15 Should I bring my laptop computer?

If you are contemplating bringing your laptop, and you use it a lot here in the States, I'd say go for it. But understand a few things first. Depending on where you are going, you may end up subjecting your computer to extreme weather conditions (heat, rain, dust, humidity, etc.). You will also be transporting it over great distances under less than ideal travel conditions (bush taxis, crowded buses, overnight trains, mami wagons, etc.). Once you get to your final destination, there may or may not be electricity, and there will almost certainly not be a repair shop in the event that it breaks down. Plus, odds are low that there will be a printer available, reliable, or interfaceable with your laptop at your post unless you end up in a big city or more developed town, so you'll need to bring your printer if you plan on printing anything.

I knew a few volunteers that brought laptops. They either had their own printers or saved all their documents to be printed at the Peace Corps office whenever they headed into the capital (once every few months). They used their computers to organize work, keep journals, make lists, play games, and so on. There were no Internet providers or local access numbers to connect to e-mail except in the capital. Even then, local phone rates to connect to the e-mail server were about as expensive as making long distance calls are here. For more on e-mail, refer to Question 46.

There were times when I wished I had brought a laptop with me just to streamline some of my work (especially grant writing for secondary projects) and store all of my diary entries. It's definitely not a necessity, but it could prove worthwhile assuming nothing goes wrong. If you have your doubts about bringing yours, you may want to leave it behind until you've scoped out your post and its amenities. Then you can have it hand-delivered by a visiting guest or a volunteer returning from homeleave.

16 Should I bring a shortwave radio?

No matter where you are going, you should bring a shortwave radio. They are easily transportable, energy efficient (some take only two to four AA batteries, which last for months under constant use), and a source of both entertainment and information when you are at your post. You'll be able to pick up local stations to tune into the culture and language, and you'll be able to pick up VOA (Voice of America) and BBC (British Broadcasting Corporation) to stay abreast of international news, including news from home.

Though I was never a big radio listener in the States, I listened to my shortwave everyday in the Peace Corps. I became familiar with the programming of stations like VOA and BBC, and found myself tuning into certain broadcasts with all the enthusiasm and dedication of an *X-Files* fan on a Sunday night in the States. Many volunteers even conceded that listening to their shortwave radios overseas helped keep them better informed of world politics and current affairs than they had been in the States.

Shortwave radios are expensive—they run about one hundred dollars for a good one—but as with Walkmans and boom boxes, the ones you buy here will be far more reliable than ones you may find overseas at comparable prices. And when you leave the Peace Corps, you can often sell your shortwave radio to an incoming volunteer or give it as a treasured gift to a friend in the village. My only advice is to shop around and don't let the cost scare you away. For the weight, it may turn out to be the best and most valuable item you bring.

17 What about the water? Will I need a purifier?

Do not worry about water. The Peace Corps will teach you all you need to know to prepare water for drinking. They will go over various methods of filtering, boiling, and purifying. You'll learn to disinfect water with chlorine bleach and other solutions. You'll also be given a ceramic candle water filter for your house, or money to buy one locally as part of your settling-in allowance.

In addition, as those of you who have traveled extensively already know, bottled water is available in almost every country in the world. Though Peace Corps volunteers usually can't afford bottled water as their primary drinking source, it suffices when they're away from post and unable to treat local water. If you have a portable (camping) water purifier, you may wish to bring it if space allows, but few volunteers use them as alternatives abound.

My strongest recommendation is to maintain vigilance in treating your drinking water throughout your service. I can't count the number of volunteers I knew who, after several months at post, abandoned their water treatment routines. Some wanted to acclimate their systems to local water as a kind of Peace Corps right-of-passage. Others were too lazy to boil and filter consistently. Others, still, falsely assumed their water source was clean due to the location of their posts. Not surprisingly, these were the same volunteers who battled strange stomach disorders and made repeated trips to the medical office for the duration of their service. Though giardia (waterborne amoebas) can usually be treated with a few pills, why expose yourself to the discomfort and health risk in the first place? The Peace Corps' methods for treating water are simple and effective.

As for bathing, I knew several volunteers who brought camping-style solar showers or had them sent, only to have them sit, unused, in their closets for the next two years. If you have a shower and running water in your house, you won't want to use the solar shower just to make the water warm. You'll either install some kind of water heater or get used to quick, cold showers. If you don't have a shower or running water, you'll take bucket baths, in which case it's just as easy to heat up your bath water on your stove before bathing.

18 Can I bring my pet overseas with me?

Unfortunately, the Peace Corps does not allow volunteers to transport their pets to their overseas assignments. Though this policy may appear unduly stern, it exists for some good reasons. First, it wouldn't be any fun for the pet, especially during your three months of intensive onsite training. Beside the fact that you will be emotionally unstable, physically stressed, and extraordinarily busy, you'll probably also be stunned at how differently (and horribly) pets are treated in most developing countries.

In addition, handling the paperwork, legalities, quarantine requirements, and costs of transporting your pet overseas would entail an immense commitment of time and resources both here and overseas. With all that's required to prepare for your trip, the added burden of preparing your pet for the trip would complicate things exponentially. Once you arrive in-country, your schedule leaves no room for tending to the responsibilities associated with pet transfers.

The good news is that many PCVs adopt pets once they've settled into village life and feel more at home in the Peace Corps. Doing so usually saves a local animal from being abused (or even eaten), and provides an instant source of distraction, entertainment, and responsibility that makes the two years pass by a little easier. For more on adopting pets in the Peace Corps, refer to Question 29.

Part III
Peace Corps Training—
Learning the Ropes

19 What is training like?

Peace Corps training is an experience in and of itself.

It is three months (give or take) of making new friends, taking new steps, learning about a different culture, and learning about yourself. It pampers you and challenges you, informs you and confuses you, allows you to grow but shelters you. Most importantly, it prepares you for two years on your own in an environment more foreign and exciting than any you've ever encountered.

Peace Corps training focuses on several critical areas to nurture you from a clueless tourist to a seasoned veteran in a short period of time. Those areas include technical training in your program (agroforestry, teaching English as a foreign language (TEFL), health, community development, etc.); language training in the national language and local dialects; health, hygiene, and safety training (important, and sometimes grotesquely fascinating); and cross-cultural/development training. Within each of those topics you'll find interesting lectures and boring ones, informative ones and redundant ones, important ones and useless ones. Most are structured using an adult education and experiential learning model, meaning they are interactive, participatory, and hands-on. Despite the fact that you may at times feel a bit cloistered, training prepares you well for the difficult transition to life at post.

For many Peace Corps programs, an integral part of training is the "homestay" experience. Soon after arriving in-country, trainees are sent to live with host families for a part, or the entire length of, the training program. Your host family will live within walking or taxi distance from the training center; they may or may not speak English; they may be extremely poor, middle class, or well off; and they may or may not have hosted a Peace Corps trainee (PCT) before. The only thing you can be sure of is that they'll have a room for you, and they will provide you with breakfast and possibly dinner, depending on their arrangements with the Peace Corps. They will be an excellent source of both cultural and linguistic immersion. You may really bond with them and keep in touch with them long after training is over; you may not. They may suffocate you, demanding to know where you are going at night and what time you'll be back for dinner (especially true for female trainees), or they may treat you like an adult, unconcerned with your schedule or your whereabouts. They may have a TV, radio, toilet, shower, and telephone, or they may have a pit latrine and no electricity.

In my training group, we had all kinds of interesting homestay experiences. Some of us were really lucky and forged close, enduring relationships with our families; others had to switch to a different homestay family two or three times before settling in. Although most homestay experiences are positive or at least bearable, if you find that your homestay experience is intolerable (i.e., you're in the most dangerous part of town, your family fails to provide you with breakfast or dinner, your room is a breeding ground for roaches and mosquitoes), ask for a transfer to a different family. You aren't stuck with the first family you get, and no one is expecting you to suffer through hell for three months in the name of "cultural sensitivity" or "personal flexibility."

Aside from the homestay experience, training itself is a rigorous and intensive few months of classes, seminars, field trips, and evaluations. The following are generalizations based on my training experience, and those of other RPCVs from various Peace Corps programs. Expect to attend classes from 8 A.M. to 5 P.M. Monday through Friday, and 8 A.M. to noon on Saturday. Language classes often comprise a big part of the morning, technical training follows in the afternoon. Lunch is provided by the training center, lasting an hour. Sandwiched in this strict timetable are weekly vaccinations, lectures on health and safety, cross-cultural and development seminars, and "homestay processing" (a forum to discuss your homestay experiences with other volunteers and trainers). In training, you work in groups and on individual projects, you are evaluated and make your own evaluations of your trainers biweekly, and you still find time to socialize and make friends.

Training really is an interesting experience in time management. My memories of training include everything from endless hours of conversation in a foreign language, to sprinting to the post office during lunch hour to send letters and buy stamps. The days are full, but so are the evenings and nights. After training, you still have to decide how to divvy up the remainder of the day. Do you go back to your homestay family and spend quality time bonding and playing with your little brothers and sisters? Do you stick around the training center to play volleyball with a group of your fellow trainees? Do you head into town to grab a bowl of beans and rice and a beer with another group of friends? Or do you go for a walk by yourself, seeking quiet time to think and process, absorb and evaluate? Somehow, over the three months of training, you'll find the time to do them all.

20 How hard will it be to learn the language? What language(s) will I learn?

The Peace Corps approach to language learning has been hailed as one of the best in the world. Rather than the conventional method of starting with vocabulary drills, verb conjugations, and personal pronoun memorization, trainees engage in direct dialogue with native speakers from day one. Before you know it, you're making connections and picking up vocab and tenses just by hearing them spoken correctly the first time around. The instructors are generally excellent, guiding you and correcting you, encouraging you and lauding your efforts regardless of your accent or speed. Every week or two you are reevaluated and placed in different groups depending on your progress. At the beginning of the day, you'll go around the room and answer basic questions like "How did you sleep?" and "Tell us something that you did last night with your homestay family." You'll get to hear how others answer and figure out ways to communicate your own thoughts so you are understood, even if you aren't "textbook" correct.

This conversational approach, learning by speaking and hearing, is punctuated with conventional lessons in grammar, tense, vocabulary, and conjugation—lessons that become enlightening interludes after struggling with sentences and wondering just how to say things like "I wish I could" during the more interactive sessions of dialogue and exchange. At the end of twelve weeks you will find yourself with a solid foundation from which to hone your foreign language skills over the next two years.

There are people who, no matter how hard they try, can't seem to progress at the rate required by the strict timetable of training. For those people, language tutors and instructors are available for after-class sessions, lunchtime course work, and one-on-one training. Granted, it's no fun to be grinding through French or Spanish while your friends are throwing a Frisbee around or writing letters in the sun, but it's Peace Corps' way of telling you that they will not let you "fail" training, so long as you have the interest and are willing to work with them.

As far as which languages you will learn, count on learning the national language first and foremost. Everyone will start out learning French, Spanish, Portuguese, Swahili, or whatever the official language may be. If your country has a predominant local language also spoken and used heavily, you'll probably be trained in that as well. Once you receive your post assignment, if there are a few weeks left in training, you may even start classes in small, local vernaculars spoken around the area where you'll be working. Peace Corps has the resources to teach you the language skills you need to function and work in your village. Take advantage of them to get a grip on the basics (at a minimum), then dive in headfirst to pick up the rest while you're out in the field.

There are often Peace Corps–sponsored language seminars offered at various points during your two years of service, as well. Those classes are designed to gauge your progress, fine-tune your language skills, and get everyone together for some fun and relaxation. I'd advise keeping an ear open for opportunities like that; they help make it all come together and make you realize how far you've come at the same time.

21 Will I have enough technical training to do my job?

Eventually, yes. The Peace Corps' technical training is a priority and is designed to provide everyone with a high level of competence. Although people from all levels of experience enter the program, each volunteer leaves training on equal ground, equipped to do his or her job for two years independent of close supervision or scrutiny.

Your technical trainers will almost always be former Peace Corps volunteers who excelled in their jobs and have an enthusiasm for their work. They are excellent resources for gaining skills you'll need in the field, and providing nontechnical information about the Peace Corps experience along the way. Technical training focuses on practical skills, as opposed to theory or policy. If you're an agro-forester, you'll spend fifty to seventy-five percent of your class time on a farm or demonstration plot getting your hands dirty. If you're a teacher, you'll spend lots of time in front of peers, students, and trainers honing your teaching skills. If you're a health worker, you'll visit clinics and hospitals, learn how to weigh babies and make soap, and practice giving speeches on health-related subjects in the local language. In many ways, once you reach your village you'll feel as though you've already racked up some experience, and won't be as intimidated as you initially anticipated.

Technical training starts with the basics, accommodating trainees who have minimal to no previous knowledge of the subject area. Over the next few months, however, the pace picks up rapidly. As with language training, if you start falling behind, you can get extra help and do additional work to catch up. You won't be trained in every aspect of your field, just in those aspects that allow you to accomplish programmatic work objectives. Peace Corps provides you with a foundation of knowledge during training to carry you through your first few weeks and months at post; from there it's your responsibility to supplement that training with hands-on, site-specific field experience.

One year into your service, Peace Corps will host a technical refresher course called In-Service Training (IST). IST provides a chance to get out of your village, reconvene with other volunteers in your program, share ideas, and learn new techniques from your associate Peace Corps director (APCD) and guest speakers (often host country national professionals). IST can be useful in many ways. Beyond formal training planned for the week, you'll pick up important tips and pointers from second-year volunteers who are nearing their close-of-service (COS) dates. Depending on how competent your APCD is, formal lectures and field demonstrations may also shed light on problems or frustrations you have encountered in your village. As with any Peace Corps gathering, IST also offers an opportunity to socialize with friends and colleagues you may not have seen in a while.

22 Will I be trained on how to repair my mountain bike / motorcycle?

As I mention in Question 31, Peace Corps may issue you a mountain bike or motorcycle once you swear in. If you receive either, you'll participate in a two- to three-day course to teach you the basics of maintenance and repair. All tools and parts will be provided, as will instruction from an experienced technician (usually a second-year volunteer or qualified host country national).

If the extent of your experience in mechanics is limited to filling your tires with air, don't fret. Peace Corps assumes you know nothing about bike or motorcycle maintenance when they train you. After the course, you should be able to keep your bike or motorcycle running, for the most part, throughout your two years. For more serious repair work, you'll be welcome to visit the Peace Corps office in the capital to acquire parts or solicit assistance from others.

Though I didn't have a motorcycle in the Peace Corps, volunteers who did informed me that their "moto-training" was comprehensive. They learned how to disassemble the entire engine, clean everything, then reassemble it. They also learned riding techniques, "emergency" repair techniques, and safety tips. In addition, the Peace Corps holds periodic refresher courses at different points during the two years to distribute new tools and ensure that everyone's motorcycles are in good running order.

Similarly, Peace Corps' mountain-bike training course is comprehensive and user-friendly, providing volunteers with the knowledge and tools to maintain their bikes for the duration of their service. Of course, once you've left the safety of the training center and bring your bike to post, it helps to put your newly acquired knowledge to use. Riding conditions for most PCVs are often harsh, taking their toll on the life span of bikes that aren't regularly maintained.

For me, it was a great pleasure on a rainy day to pull out my repair manual, lay my tools out on the floor, pop in a good tape, and spend hours tending to my mountain bike. I learned a lot about performing advanced tune-ups, replacing complex parts, and doing serious repair work that way. I'd recommend taking advantage of the two years to teach yourself these practical skills, too.

Part IV
Managing Your Money

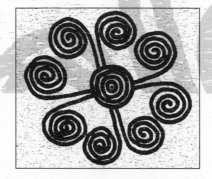

23 How will I get paid? Where will I keep my money?

The Peace Corps pays its volunteers either monthly or quarterly, depending on where you serve. Once every pay period a check will be mailed to your local post office box by registered mail, or you'll have a check deposited directly into a local (Peace Corps contracted) bank account. In countries or villages where there are no stable banks, or the mail system is completely dysfunctional, someone from the office will travel to each region where volunteers are posted and distribute living allowances by hand. In other cases still, if you know you'll be coming into the Peace Corps office for medical or other purposes around the time that checks are being cut, you can have your administrative officer hold the check and pick it up yourself.

The way you store your money is up to you. If you have an account at an accessible, reputable, and reliable bank, you can keep it there. The bank may be in your town or village, or it may be in a nearby town which you visit every few weeks to stock up on supplies, visit other volunteers, and run errands. As long as you, other volunteers, and the Peace Corps administration have confidence in the bank and its operations, this option is generally the safest and easiest.

If you are wary of the banking system, or are too far from a reputable bank to make practical use of it, you can cash your check every pay period and hide the money in your house. Keep in mind, however, the dangers involved in managing your money this way. House break-ins and Peace Corps robberies can be common, and if word gets around that a stash of money is hidden in your house, you may find your house becoming an even bigger target than it already is. It may also be hard to budget yourself if your whole paycheck is available to you at all times. Volunteers who have to travel to a bank or some other secure location (the Peace Corps office, etc.) to withdraw funds usually stretch their living allowances out better than those who can dip into it at any time.

If you hide your money in your house, take extra care not to let anyone, including your best friend, trusted house help, neighbor, landlord, and the multitude of seemingly innocent kids who come around every day to play, see where your hiding place is. We had one instance in my program where a volunteer was spied taking money from her cache by the ten-year-old son of her neighbor. Though he never stole any of it, he disclosed the hiding place to his classmates and the following week almost $600 was missing.

If you are robbed, you can turn to the Peace Corps for "emergency funds" to carry you over until the next pay period. Sometimes, though, they may deduct those funds from future living allowance checks. They may also take it out of your readjustment allowance—money set aside for your completion of service, typically amounting to $225 for every month served, to use as you like. Regardless, you'll need to go to the Peace Corps office, file a theft report, and talk to your program director and administrative officer. The bottom line: think carefully about how and where you keep your money and other valuables; you are already a target simply by virtue of the fact that you are a foreigner. Don't make the target bigger if you can help it.

24 Will I have enough money? Should I bring extra money with me?

Yes, you will have enough money to live comfortably wherever you serve. By "comfortably" I mean you will have enough to eat balanced meals, go out for drinks, travel around, buy crafts and souvenirs, have clothes made, buy toiletries, give gifts and contributions at social functions, go to dinner and a movie when you're in the capital, and so on. Although the Peace Corps tries hard to promote a grassroots volunteer lifestyle, and encourages you to "live at the level of your neighbors in the village," they have to balance that philosophy with the reality of keeping you healthy, happy, and productive. In other words, unless your neighbors are high-ranking government officials or successful businesspeople, you will generally be much better off than most of those around you at the village level.

Though I can't tell you exactly how much your living allowance will be, PCVs in Cameroon received roughly $270 per month. Other countries' living allowances vary based on local prices and inflation, volunteer feedback (from periodic surveys), and the Peace Corps' annual budget. Living allowances may also differ from region to region within a given country, reflecting relative price differences in basic commodities, housing, and so on. If local economic conditions deteriorate substantially during your service, your allowance may change while you are overseas to compensate. Suffice it to say, I knew of very few volunteers who found their allowances to be insufficient to cover their everyday costs in the Peace Corps.

There may, however, be times when you find yourself short on cash due to events or expenses that are above and beyond your normal budget. Perhaps you take an extended vacation or purchase an expensive souvenir. In those instances don't fret, you can always borrow from a fellow PCV, cash in a traveler's check or some American dollars if you brought some, or in real dire straits explain your situation to the Peace Corps administration to receive emergency funds or an advance on your next living allowance check. One way or another, you'll be covered.

The only other time during your service when you may not have enough money is during training. In training, since you aren't yet a volunteer, you receive a weekly stipend rather than the standard living allowance. As Peace Corps provides you with housing, meals, snacks, and a full schedule of classes and sessions to keep you busy, they don't anticipate that you'll need much spending money during training. You'll find, however, once you start exploring the area and discovering local bars, restaurants, and markets, you'll wish you had more than fourteen dollars per week in your pockets (that was the amount my training group received). For those initial months, I'd recommend bringing some American dollars or travelers checks to exchange for local currency. Cash will always fetch you a better rate than checks, and there is no fee for changing cash, so bring bills— the bigger the better (currency exchange businesses often prefer to deal with fifty-dollar bills or higher). A couple hundred dollars provides a nice cushion, and, if you don't spend it during training, you'll appreciate the backup funds during lean months or special occasions that arise over the next two years.

Part V
Living Like the Locals

25 Will I live in a mud hut? Will I have electricity or running water?

These are typical questions that everyone who is thinking of joining the Peace Corps ponders. The answer is simple, but a bit frustrating: it depends. Before I get into a discussion about why it depends, let me present some relevant statistics from the *1997 Peace Corps Volunteer Survey Report*, produced by the Peace Corps Office of Planning, Policy and Analysis (Oct. 1, 1997, p. 24):

> *Electricity:* Only 25% of all [PCV] respondents lived with no electricity, another 25% had electricity sometimes, and 50% always had electricity.
>
> • Regional differences in access to any electricity ranged from 98% in ECAM [Europe/ Central Asia/ Mediterranean], 88% in IA [Inter-America], and 84% in the Pacific and Asia, to 46% in Africa.
>
> • In the business sector, 94% of the respondents had electricity at least sometimes, while only 53% of those working in agriculture and 57% of those in health projects had electricity at least sometimes.
>
> *Running water:* Worldwide, 42% of the respondents had a reliable source of running water, 30% sometimes had running water, and 28% never had running water.
>
> • The exception was Africa where only 41% of the respondents had running water at least sometimes, compared with 95% in ECAM, 83% in the Pacific, 82% in IA and 78% in Asia.
>
> • Sector differences were similar to those for electricity—respondents in the business sector were at the high end of the scale at 91% with at least some running water, while only 51% in agriculture, and 50% of those in health, ever had running water.

With regards to housing, the survey had the following to report (p. 16):

Living arrangements: Only 18% of respondents worldwide lived with host-country families. The exception was Asia where 35% lived with families. In addition, 27% of the respondents from the agriculture sector lived with families.

Allow me to shed some light on those statistics. Within the developing world, countries vary greatly in their level of development and the extent of their infrastructure. In Africa, for example, you'll find that some countries (Guinea, Niger, Mali) are much less "developed" than others (the Ivory Coast, Kenya, South Africa). This disparity in economic wealth is reflected in the quantity and quality of their roads, telephone lines, access to electricity and running water, and construction of houses and buildings. If you are assigned to a country that has a relatively developed infrastructure, your chances of having running water and electricity in your village are greater than if you are sent to a severely depressed or less developed nation.

Your living conditions also depend on where you are posted within your country. You may find that there are certain regions that are better off than others. If you are assigned to a village in a more developed area of your country, you'll often find that there is electricity and running water. Also, the roads in those areas tend to be better (sometimes even paved), and phone lines are more plentiful. Villages in the food-producing regions, the touristy spots, and the areas just outside the provincial capitals may be much more modern than villages located in the heart of the undeveloped parts of the country (rain forests, deserts, mountains).

Generally, your program administrator will ask for your preferences regarding water/electricity/housing toward the end of training, before they assign you to a post. Which isn't to say your input will always be taken into consideration, but at least you'll have an opportunity to express your desires and hope for the best. Oftentimes a certain group of people will adamantly insist that they want a village without electricity or running water, while another group will prioritize those amenities, and almost everyone will end up getting what they want without competition.

I had both electricity and running water in my village, and

though at times I felt like perhaps I wasn't getting the complete "bush experience," overall I realized that spending two years immersed in another country, language, and culture was, in many ways, exotic and challenging enough. In fact, I enjoyed using my cassette player without buying cartons of batteries, washing my dishes and taking showers without hauling water from the stream, and reading at night to a light source that wasn't blackening my ceiling (and lungs) with kerosene smoke. Neither my electricity nor my taps were entirely reliable—they were out of service sporadically throughout my service (sometimes for hours, sometimes for weeks)—but their capricious quality only deepened my appreciation for them.

As for having your own house, most volunteers live by themselves for their two years overseas. If a house isn't set up and waiting when you arrive in your village, it is within reason to request that one be prepared for you. In some cases, you may have to look around yourself to discover which houses are available to rent. In others, you may need to have a house built for you, and stay with a neighboring family or colleague while it's being constructed. If there's a Peace Corps rest house nearby, you may be able to stay there temporarily, as well. In most cases, however, Peace Corps will have researched the housing situation in your village well before your arrival, and arranged with local leaders and counterparts to have something ready and waiting by the time you arrive. Expenses associated with establishing housing are covered by the Peace Corps, either as rent included in your living allowance, or supplemental payment on an individual basis covering construction or remodeling costs (within reason).

If you prefer to stay with a homestay family in your village or live in a compound with your neighbors, you are welcome to do so. If you are posted to an extremely small village, for example, you may find it both impractical and culturally insensitive to live by yourself. Volunteers I knew who lived with families had rich and rewarding experiences, and often felt closer to the culture and society in which they served.

living like the locals

26 How will I wash my clothes? Do my dishes? Clean my house?

If you're into it, do it yourself. If not, hire someone. Peace Corps volunteers routinely hire locals to clean, cook, and wash for them. Don't gasp—it's not as paternalistic or colonial as it may sound. It's offering someone in your village a job with wages that will pay their way through school or afford them the means of purchasing medicine for their children. In fact, when word gets out that you are in search of a house helper, there will be a line outside your door that winds around the village block.

Granted, not every volunteer hires a helper. I knew a few that were intent on washing every article of clothing, carrying every bucket of water, scrubbing every inch of floor space, and cooking every meal themselves for their entire two years. Of course, they were hounded regularly by kids, neighbors, acquaintances, and total strangers who were pleading for work and insisting that they could do a better job for a small salary. I do realize that some people just aren't comfortable with the idea of having a "maid" or "cook" care for them and their house—especially in the Peace Corps—but many volunteers think of it as an opportunity to provide an individual in the village with income, which is exactly what it is.

If you do decide to hire someone, there are a couple of arrangements you can make with that person. Many Peace Corps houses have annexes or back rooms in which a live-in housekeeper can stay, free of charge, on the condition that they do the agreed-upon chores and look over the house (and any pets) in the volunteer's absence. Oftentimes, if you have a live-in housekeeper, you'll end up forming a friendship with that person and his/her family that will quickly transcend the worker/supervisor relationship that first existed. On the other hand, there have been cases where live-in house help have robbed PCVs, or taken advantage of the situation to violate the PCV's privacy in his/her absence. If you decide on the live-in arrangement, try to find someone who has worked with Peace Corps volunteers in the past (odds are they'll find you first, anyway), and don't be afraid to ask other volunteers in the area and friends of yours in the village about the applicant's character.

Other volunteers hire someone to come by once every week or

two for a full day of sweeping, washing, dusting, and drying. That arrangement may be more convenient and sensible if you keep your house clean for the most part and only want help with the down-and-dirty scrubbing and washing. As with the live-in arrangement, check references and ask around before agreeing to hire someone to work for you on a part-time basis. Keep in mind, too, that in most villages in the developing world, there is no obsession with punctuality and scheduling as there is in America. If you've agreed with your house help to meet up in two weeks for another cleaning session, and the person shows up two hours late or not at all, there may be a myriad of reasons that are all perfectly acceptable and legitimate in that culture. So unless it gets out of hand, don't let it frustrate you. You'll find that to be true not just with your house help, but with your work in the Peace Corps in general.

27 What is the food like?

Local foods differ depending on the country, the region, and the local culture. Some volunteers, for example, are posted in areas where meat is abundant, but fruits and vegetables are scarce. For others, the opposite is true. Often you'll find familiar basic ingredients prepared in unfamiliar ways. Regardless of where you serve, however, be prepared to encounter new foods and dishes that may, at first, strike you as odd. Whether it's crocodile stew or fried grubs, you'll have the opportunity to find out just how different people's conceptions of food can be.

Aside from village fare, which may strike you as delicious, monotonous, or simply strange, you'll quickly discover the "hot spots" in bigger towns and the capital city where you can go once in a while for more familiar dishes—burgers, fries, pizza, or banana splits. Don't count on frequenting those restaurants, as they are usually priced for tourists, expatriates, and wealthy HCNs, but take heart in knowing that every country has at least a few places where you'll be able to satisfy the occasional craving for American cooking.

Though I can't tell you exactly what the food will be like in your area, if you keep an open mind and get excited to try new and different cuisines, you'll probably come back to the States two years down the road with cravings for that village dish that you can't find anywhere else in the world. If it turns out that you can't stand anything prepared locally, don't fret—as I mention in Question 34, you'll have the means and time to create your own, more familiar dishes to get you through.

28 What if I'm a vegetarian?

True to the stereotype, many Peace Corps volunteers are vegetarian, and many who are not convert once they arrive overseas. You shouldn't have a problem preparing nutritious and balanced meals if you are a vegetarian, but you should pay careful attention to your protein intake. As I mention in Question 32, most Peace Corps countries host a panoply of diseases that your body isn't accustomed to battling. Allowing yourself to become protein-deficient increases your vulnerability to those diseases. Most protein in developing countries comes from fish, meat, and/or beans. If you don't eat fish or meat, and you don't like beans, you may be in trouble.

Depending on where you serve, you may find a wide variety of farm-fresh vegetables and handpicked fruits available at your local market. These foods are often grown organically, with no fertilizers or pesticides, and harvested within a day or two of the time you eat them. In the States you'd pay premium prices at specialty grocery stores for the kinds of produce you'll find at some Peace Corps posts.

You may be wondering why meat-eaters would be inclined to become vegetarian once they join the Peace Corps. In many cases it's because they are posted to remote villages where the only meats available are taken from surrounding forests and savannah—animals like monkey, bat, and antelope—and they don't care for the taste or idea of eating them. In other cases, they visit the market in their villages and see the proverbial cow head and body parts hanging from hooks in the open air, flies and other bugs gorging freely. Others find that the price of meat in their village is exorbitant, perhaps because it is imported from faraway towns (probably transported in less than sterile conditions, to boot).

The only sticky situation you may encounter if you're a vegetarian in the Peace Corps is the occasional meal at a friend or colleague's house where meat is bought, prepared, and offered to you as a gesture of hospitality. In those instances, it can be incredibly awkward to explain that you don't eat meat for moral, health, or taste reasons. Your hosts will have spent precious money on the meat and will probably have placed the best portion on your plate. Vegetarian friends of mine who found themselves in those situations usually bit the bullet and ate. Others obsequiously deferred to religious excuses ("My religion forbids me from eating meat; I am terribly sorry but I deeply appreciate the trouble you have gone through to make me feel welcome," or something like that) to get out of the predicament—the only excuse that may actually work.

It's worth noting that, in some countries and regions, vegetarian PCVs have been known to forgo their habitual diets and start eating meat again. In Eastern Europe and parts of sub-Saharan Africa, meat dishes are prepared so well and are so enticing, even stalwart vegetarians occasionally throw in the flag. Fruits and vegetables in those areas are often too scarce or too costly to serve as the basis for balanced and nutritious meals, compounding the pressure to eat meat. But don't let that scare you. Committed and resourceful vegetarians, no matter where they are posted, can usually find ways to stick to their diets if they wish.

29 Can I buy or adopt a pet overseas?

Absolutely. In fact, Peace Corps pets are a valuable and integral part of the experience for many volunteers. They keep you company, they keep you busy, and they usually keep you a bit safer at post. If you get a cat, it will chase away mice and rid your house of roaches and spiders. If you get a dog, it will alert you to visitors and guard your house when you are away. Some volunteers get so attached to their pets, they bring them back to the States after their service is over (see Question 72).

I had a cat, and though I've never considered myself to be much of a "cat person," I can't imagine having gone through my two years without her. She was affectionate and playful, and was an adept mouser. She had at least five litters over two years, and I gave all the kittens away to other volunteers. I found that having a cat was practical for many reasons. She definitely provided me with constant company, but she was also easy to feed and clean. I set up a litter box for her in my "supply room," fed her dried fish and rice from the market (which cost me around one dollar per week), and had my parents send me a few flea collars. After I left I passed her on to my replacement and, last I heard, she's healthy and happy and continuing to supply volunteers with new kittens.

A good number of my Peace Corps friends had dogs—village pups that they acquired as gifts from neighbors or colleagues. Dogs are great Peace Corps pets, but are high maintenance. They tend to get dirtier, cause more trouble (chasing local goats, chickens, and kids), require more training, and need more attention than cats. Plus, dogs need babysitters when you leave your post for extended periods, whereas cats are virtually self-sufficient.

The upside of having a dog, as any dog-lover will tell you, is that they shower more unconditional love on you, and can provide you with more company than some of your best human friends. They may also be better security guards than your neighbors or house help. As I mentioned above, most volunteers in my area who had dogs became so attached to them they considered bringing them back to the States. The same wasn't true for those with pet cats.

30 How will my neighbors and colleagues view me?

This depends, in large part, on where you serve. In general, however, you'll find that Peace Corps' reputation as an effective, motivated, committed, and dynamic development organization is unsurpassed. The longer Peace Corps has served in a particular country, the more widespread and positive its reputation. Since volunteers serve at the grassroots level, while Peace Corps administration works directly with government officials, rich politicians and poor farmers alike become familiar with the organization. As a result, volunteers are often welcomed by their counterparts and neighbors, and are treated with respect by those they encounter wherever they venture during their two years overseas.

Of course, there are occasions when Peace Corps' reputation seems a bit less inviolate. Some government officials may perceive Peace Corps volunteers as obtrusive foreigners who flaunt their immunity to local customs (translated: refuse to pay bribes during certain transactions). Some villagers and local townspeople may regard volunteers as spoiled Americans with misplaced values—rich enough to forsake high-paying job opportunities in the States, and callous enough to abandon their families for two years. Others may have been exposed to PCVs in social scenes, and reached the conclusion that volunteers are nothing more than drunken socialites. But those "bad raps" are few and far between in comparison to the impression of PCVs as devoted, culturally sensitive, and uniquely giving members of the development community. With that in mind, your job will be easier if you do your part to uphold the positive aspects of Peace Corps' reputation, or establish it if it hasn't already been established in your village.

What you may find surprising, regardless of where you serve, is the degree to which American culture has invaded the developing world. From the highlands of Nepal to the deserts of sub-Saharan Africa, you'll find Michael Jackson T-shirts, Dolly Parton cassettes, blue jeans, soap operas, and other random fragments of Americana on proud display in local shops and markets. Without a deeper understanding of this country and all its intricacies, many people in the developing world infer from those images that Americans are rich, powerful, socially aggressive people. Even if your neighbors and colleagues have no clue about the Peace Corps, when they discover you are an American they will make assumptions about you based on the stereotypes proffered by our exported pop culture. Though the assumptions may be laughably inaccurate, in most cases they'll be harmless and entertaining foundations from which you can educate the people who judge you by them.

31 How will I travel around my work area?

It used to be that every Peace Corps volunteer (or nearly every one) was issued a motorcycle after training as a means of traveling to work sites and maximizing work productivity and efficiency. Then someone compiled statistics on the leading causes of Peace Corps deaths and discovered that the number one killer of PCVs was, lo and behold, motorcycle accidents. Everything from drunk moto riding to hitting a coconut or a goat doing thirty on a dirt road was to blame. So began the moto phaseout which, I believe, is near completion.

In other words, don't count on getting a motorcycle unless you have an outstanding reason based on the location of your post and workload. It also helps if you possess a U.S. motorcycle driver's license, but even then it's a hard sell. More than likely, if you are in a program that requires you to travel to various work sites and villages, you will be issued a mountain bike. Initially, Peace Corps gave volunteers forty-pound Huffys with no tools. Today, volunteers can look forward to receiving a relatively new (maybe second or third-hand) mid-level Trek, Nishiki, or something similar. You'll get a complete set of tools, a saddle bag, a pump, a water bottle, a helmet, a front and rear light, extra parts, and a manual on how to fix and maintain your bike. You'll also attend a mandatory two- to three-day bike class to learn the basics of assembly, maintenance, and riding (see Question 22).

Aside from the obvious exercise and health benefits, odds are you'll be the only person in your village with such a funky-looking bike, able to climb steep and rutted hills and descend faster than your average goat. It'll be a conversation piece and a head-turner. It'll get you in good with the kids in your village (who will stand and stare at it for hours while you're teaching your class or working your farms), and will provoke smiles, nods, and thumbs-up signs as you cruise through the center of town on your way back home. Also, most Peace Corps posts offer excellent mountain-bike riding opportunities—single-track galore and dirt roads everywhere! People in the States drive for hours with their bikes on top of their cars to find terrain like that!

If you are one of the chosen few issued a motorcycle, all of the above will hold true for you, too. You will be provided with tools, a helmet, gloves, a manual, and instruction on how to fix your machine, how to take it apart, and how to put it back together again. It will also turn heads in the village, though sometimes for the wrong reasons. Most people have seen motorcycles (more than have seen mountain bikes), but in the third world motorcycles are usually equated with wealth. So look out; if you have a motorcycle, people are less likely to understand the "volunteer living at the level of the villager" concept. Also, be prepared to endure endless demands for rides to the market, trips to the hospital, and lifts to the farm. Of course, there are benefits to having a motorcycle: you can cover more ground in much less time; you aren't held to the erratic and sometimes nonexistent schedules of local bush taxis or buses; and it's more fun going uphill, especially on those hot and dusty days of the dry season.

You should also be prepared for the possibility that you will get neither a bike nor a motorcycle! Although most Peace Corps countries issue some form of transportation to their volunteers, there are those that encourage you to let your feet do the walking. Reasons include terrain, location of posts, program requirements, etc. Once you find out where you are going, call Peace Corps or read through the materials they send you to see what they say on this topic. In Cameroon, agroforestry, fish, health, and community development volunteers had bikes or motorcycles. Education volunteers (both TEFL and math/science) didn't get anything because it was expected that they would live close to their schools, obviating the need for an improved means of reaching their work sites or covering more territory. Certain education volunteers that really wanted bikes, however, successfully petitioned their program directors and requisitioned those old forty-pound Huffys that were lying around the office—so there is hope!

Part VI
Common Medical and
Safety Concerns

32 Will I get sick?

Yes, you will get sick. As with my response to "Will I be lonely?," irrespective of where you are or what you're doing in any given two-year period, you are guaranteed to get sick at least a few times. The difference, and the real worry, is whether or not you'll be sick for the whole two years (or for a good part of it). Being in a developing country often means exposing yourself to a host of weird diseases, parasites, and ailments, which can be very discouraging for someone who otherwise really wants to join the Peace Corps. Not to mention the ways it can affect your family's support of your decision to join the Peace Corps.

The reality is, you will be inoculated against lots of terrifying diseases. You will receive extensive training on how to avoid contracting everything from filaria to malaria. You will, at first, be adamant about staying clean and healthy, determined to defy the odds. Then you'll come down with something—maybe amoebas, maybe bacterial dysentery, maybe a tumbo worm, or something as benign as a chigger (a mite that causes itching). At that point, the first step on your path toward a more relaxed (and realistic) outlook on getting sick will be taken. Over time, you'll realize how pointless it is to be paranoid about everything you touch and eat. You'll also realize that, using common sense, it is possible to *minimize* the risks to your health. Then you'll relax and spend two years marveling at the ways your body handles some pretty strange things.

I was one of the most anal volunteers around when it came to hygiene and attempts to ward off the diseases that commonly afflicted my fellow PCVs. I washed my hands before every meal, I let my clothes dry for three days before wearing them (to kill any mango-fly eggs), I boiled and filtered my water, I took my malaria prophylaxis religiously, I soaked my veggies in iodine before eating them, and so on. Yet, within my two years, I still managed to get giardiasis, bacterial dysentery, amoebas, malaria, chiggers, tumbo worms, fevers, diarrhea, and strange bites, marks, scratches, and rashes that came and went with the winds. I'm not trying to scare you; I only wish to convey to you how common, bearable, and in many ways unavoidable getting sick in the Peace Corps is. In fact, PCVs often perceive illnesses as more of an inconvenience and a hot topic of conversation than anything else.

You will not be sick every day for two years, nor will you look back when you COS and think, "If it weren't for all those diseases, I would have had a great experience." More than likely, you'll come to accept various medical problems as part of life in the Peace Corps. You shouldn't let your guard down when it comes to hygiene and health care, right up until your last day in-country, but you shouldn't fret now over what may be later—when you do get sick overseas, you'll see that it isn't the end of the world, and it certainly isn't the end of your Peace Corps service . . . or at least it needn't be.

33   Will I get worms?

I stuck this question in only because, upon returning to the States, so many people asked me if I had worms while I was in the Peace Corps. Plenty of prospective volunteers have also expressed a wary, inquisitive fascination with the topic. Proud tales of surviving intestinal parasites are plentiful in many Peace Corps countries, but not all. Your odds of getting worms are dependent, in large part, on where you are posted. In Africa, South and Central America, and Asia you may get a worm or two during your service. I managed to get through my two years worm-free, but plenty of my fellow PCVs had their day in the sun with lab results in hand and a look of horror on their face. For those who are considering joining the Peace Corps, but are particularly worried about (and discouraged by the thought of) getting worms, take heart in the fact that there are plenty of common-sense things you can do to protect yourself from ever having to deal with this.

Here are some quick-and-easy tidbits to keep in mind while you're over there. Most people learn this the hard way. Be sure to wash your hands each and every time before you eat. The most common way to get stomach worms is to have dirt under your fingernails. That dirt, particularly in developing countries, can contain worm larvae invisible to the eye. If you don't wash your hands and keep your nails trimmed, you can easily ingest the larvae as you eat, and they'll gestate in your belly. Also, wash and soak in iodine any fresh fruits and vegetables you don't intend to cook before eating.

If you do get worms, don't panic. There are various kinds of worms out there, but most can be taken care of with a few pills. You may suspect you have worms if you notice a prolonged change in appetite, loss of energy, problems with bowel movements, gas, etc. All you'll need to do is visit the Peace Corps medical office; they'll run the required tests and prescribe the appropriate medicine. Consider it another character-building life experience to brag about when you get home.

If you find yourself overly paranoid about (or sickly fascinated with) the thought of getting worms, don't worry about it—this whole topic will be dealt with thoroughly in your three months of in-country training. As I mention above, there are things you can do to minimize your chances of getting worms. Many volunteers successfully complete their service without playing host to an uninvited invertebrate. If you do get them, as with most other ailments common in the Peace Corps, it won't be as big a deal as you think it will be. I promise.

34 Will I lose weight? Gain weight?

If you ask this question of returned volunteers, you'll probably hear the same thing no matter where they served—men tend to lose weight, women tend to gain weight in the Peace Corps. Why is this? Perhaps because in most developing countries, local diets are high in starch and carbohydrates (i.e., main courses usually feature yams, potatoes, corn, bread, cassava, noodles, millet, etc.). The prevailing Peace Corps old wives' tale contends that men metabolize starches and carbos more quickly and efficiently than women, whose bodies tend to store them as fats. Whether this checks out scientifically, I don't know. Others assert that male volunteers in developing countries are given more leeway to engage in activities that are physically demanding, while females are pampered and encouraged to let men handle strenuous chores for them. Either way, most men in my program did lose weight (including me), while most women put on a few pounds.

Regardless of small weight fluctuations, the important thing to keep in mind is that it's best to stay aware of your diet, and try to keep it balanced whenever possible. There may be times when you're working in the field, sweaty and hungry, and the local women present you with a steaming mound of corn meal and small bowl of oily greens. There's no sense in denying the food or hospitality just to stick to a balanced diet, but be aware that two months of eating only food like that will take its toll on your body and health.

With regard to preparing your own meals, I know of very few Peace Corps posts around the world that don't have at least a few basic ingredients available to help you plan a balanced diet. In some regions, you may have to stock up in town and haul bulk beans and rice and canned milk back to the village with you. In other places, these staples may be available in your local village market. In either case, depending on their availability, some items may seem relatively expensive. Just remember that without your health, it will be hard to enjoy any of your Peace Corps experience, so go ahead and splurge.

The most control you'll have over your diet will be the meals you cook at home. Eating out, even at shacks and friends' houses in the village, is great once in a while—especially if the village fare is tasty (which it often is). But if you don't already know how to cook, pay attention when you get together with other, more culinarily inclined volunteers and watch how they prepare spaghetti sauce, fajitas, and vegetable stews. You may not leave Peace Corps with gourmet cooking skills, but you can leave with a talent for making good, healthy meals out of raw ingredients and spices.

35 What medical services will be available to me?

This is an important question, and one that most prospective volunteers and their families want answered clearly. As you can imagine, the Peace Corps isn't interested in sending healthy volunteers overseas, only to have them return with debilitating illnesses or injuries. Instead, they have a four-tiered system for ensuring that all volunteers are placed in safe environments and given adequate medical training and services.

First, the Peace Corps screens all applicants to identify any preexisting medical conditions or requirements which either preclude them from joining or necessitate special placement (see Appendix E, page 148). If, for example, you are allergic to bees, you may be disqualified from serving in tropical regions and therefore be sent to some place like Hungary or Nepal. This minimizes the chances that you'll aggravate an existing or known potential health problem while you're overseas.

Second, the Peace Corps hires certified doctors, nurses, nurse practitioners, and physicians' assistants to staff their field offices. This means that, in every country Peace Corps serves, there will be at least one of the above-mentioned medical personnel stationed at the Peace Corps office whose sole job is to see to the medical needs of volunteers. There may also be a roving area Peace Corps medical officer, based out of a centrally located Peace Corps office, who travels to a number of countries in their region to offer specialized services and medical care.

To be perfectly frank, you'll hear from some RPCVs that the quality of services provided by these Peace Corps doctors and nurses around the world is questionable. In fact, there are more than a few horror stories that portray the Peace Corps' medical field staff as incompetent and inexperienced. Unfortunately, some of the stories are true. But to the organization's credit, medical personnel are always available to address your health and safety concerns in-country, and to ensure that you receive treatment when necessary.

The third tier of the Peace Corps' medical program is integrated into their training program. During your three months of training, you'll spend a few hours each week learning ways to avoid contracting all kinds of diseases, parasites, and illnesses. You'll learn how to properly prepare your food and water, how to maintain good hygiene, and how to ensure personal safety at all times. You will be made aware of the gamut of possible ailments that can affect you, and you will be told how to treat those ailments yourself, when possible. At the end of the training program, you will be issued a medical kit ("med kit"), containing a first aid manual, various over-the-counter drugs (aspirin, cortisone, Bacitracin, Tums, Sudafed, etc.), bandages, syringes, and the like. If you are in a malaria-endemic country, you'll be given prophylaxes (mefloquine, doxycycline, or chloroquine) and curatives (Fansidar). You'll also be given a bountiful supply of condoms—enough to build your own raft and sail around the world with. In addition, you may receive the book *Where There Is No Doctor*, an illustrated owner's manual for the human body.

The fourth and last tier is referred to in Peace Corps jargon as "medivac." It stands for medical evacuation—a procedure for dealing with PCVs whose illnesses or injuries cannot be reasonably treated in-country. Medivacked volunteers are flown to the nearest country where adequate medical services and equipment exist. Often that country ends up being the United States, in which case the volunteer is sent directly to Washington, D.C.

If you are medivacked, the Peace Corps medical staff in Washington will review your file to determine when, if at all, you may return to your country of service. The quicker your recovery time, the better your odds of picking up where you left off. In some instances, you may be presented with the choice of returning to your post or resigning from the Peace Corps (called "medically separated" by the Peace Corps administration). In others, you may automatically be medically separated by the Peace Corps' Office of Medical Services, based on their determination of your condition (though you can appeal to the medical director in Washington, D.C.). An example of the latter would be a knee injury that requires reconstructive surgery and nine months of intensive rehabilitation. Again, much depends on the reasons for your medivac and the time frame for your recovery.

36 What if I become too sick to reach help?

This is a question that beleaguers many prospective volunteers and stirs fear in the hearts of their families. What if, one fateful day in your village, you are struck with some loathsome, mortal disease and impaired to the point where you can't even cry for assistance, let alone get treatment? What if you fall so ill, you can't endure the nine-hour donkey ride to civilization and you die a lonely death in the middle of nowhere?

For discussions on getting sick and using the Peace Corps' medical services, refer to relevant sections above. In truth, most PCVs experience little or no difficulty getting treatment when they need it. In the extremely rare instance when a volunteer is too sick to seek help, and the medicines in the Peace Corps' med kit aren't effective, that individual will be transported to a local hospital or clinic by friends or neighbors. From there, the Peace Corps medical office will be contacted. I can think of no realistic combination of circumstances that would result in a volunteer falling sick and suffering alone in his/her village, untreated for a long enough period to have something life-threatening occur. One way or another, that person would administer self-treatment, be treated locally, transport him or herself to the PC clinic, or be transported to a clinic by other volunteers or local friends.

Keep in mind that, in the Peace Corps, you are far from inconspicuous. If you go even a day without speaking to neighbors or being seen in the market, people start to wonder and worry. Friends and colleagues will always stop by your house to greet you and bring gifts—even after you've been in the village for a year. You will also be familiar enough with the local communications network to know how to reach someone in case of an emergency. Living in a fishbowl has its disadvantages, but being isolated in a time of need is not one of them.

common medical and safety concerns

37

What if I get pregnant or impregnate someone while I'm in the Peace Corps?

More volunteers than you might think have had to deal with this issue at some point during their service. The procedure varies, depending on the circumstances. Only a few constants apply, which are 1) the Peace Corps medical officer (PCMO) and country director (CD) must be notified once the pregnancy is discovered; and 2) volunteers who carry their pregnancies to term must discontinue their Peace Corps service, as Peace Corps policy precludes individuals with dependent children from serving as volunteers. That said, here are a few scenarios and the Peace Corps' policies for dealing with them:

A. **A female volunteer gets pregnant, but decides to have an abortion:**

The volunteer is allowed to fly home, have the abortion, then return to her country of service once she has recovered (with permission from the Peace Corps Medical Office in Washington, D.C.). Neither the round-trip flight nor the medical procedure, however, are paid for by the Peace Corps.

B. **A female volunteer gets pregnant and decides to carry the pregnancy to term:**

1) If she decides to deliver the child in the States, she is medically separated (see Question 33) and flown back to D.C. at the Peace Corps' expense. From there, all medical costs associated with the pregnancy are her own responsibility. If she decides to return to her country of service (perhaps to be with the father of the child), she must do so independently of the Peace Corps.

2) If she decides to give birth in-country (not a common scenario, but perhaps the dad is a host country national and the Peace Corps has determined that local medical facilities meet certain standards), she will most likely be "field separated." This means her volunteer contract with the Peace Corps is terminated but she is allowed to continue living abroad if she wishes. Otherwise, she may

continue serving as a volunteer until delivery if the CD determines that all programmatic and administrative standards can be maintained.

C. A male volunteer impregnates a host country national and acknowledges paternal ties:

The Peace Corps encourages the volunteer to provide support to the mother and child as part of his paternal responsibilities. The volunteer may be administratively separated, however, if his ability to fulfill his work requirements is hindered, or if the Peace Corps' credibility is diminished by the incident. The same is true if the volunteer has violated host country laws or customs by impregnating the HCN.

D. A male volunteer impregnates a host country national, but doesn't acknowledge paternal ties:

The Peace Corps does not get involved unless, as mentioned above, the volunteer's ability to work and maintain his program's credibility are adversely affected, in which case he may be administratively separated.

Under "extenuating circumstances," the above policies may not apply or may be modified on a case-by-case basis, but what I have outlined is what one can normally expect in those scenarios. My advice—make use of the Peace Corps' free condoms and avoid the scene altogether.

38 Is AIDS a big concern for Peace Corps volunteers?

This is a heavy topic, and one that is dealt with thoroughly during training and subsequent ISTs. Soon after you arrive in-country, you'll be shown a video featuring interviews of five returned volunteers who contracted the AIDS virus while serving overseas. All of them were infected by host country nationals. Several of them had their partners tested and were tested themselves at the Peace Corps medical office at some point during their two years. In each of those cases the tests came back negative, which the volunteers took as license to abandon the use of contraceptives (condoms). But, as it turned out, either the tests failed to account for the "six-month window" or their partners were unfaithful after they were tested. In any case, they all had AIDS and the video serves as an effective eye-opener.

The medical office will literally shower you with condoms during your service. Trojans are stuffed into your med kit and are available by the handful at the office. In many countries, condoms can be bought locally, too. If you decide to engage in sexual activities with a host country national, the office recommends having him/her tested and being adamant about using contraceptives even if you both are HIV negative. The same is true if you decide to engage in sexual activities with other PCVs, but since the AIDS rate is often exponentially higher in some developing countries, the risks can be greater if you're with a host country national.

If you are infected with HIV, you will immediately be medivacked for counseling and treatment in D.C. My advice to you is simply this: be extra careful, and extra aware, of all STDs while you are a volunteer. There may be times when you are lonely, drunk, romanced, pressured into compromising situations, or all of the above simultaneously. Don't ever let your guard down, and don't ever assume that your partner is "safe." The means to protect yourself will be everywhere—use them and avoid turning a two-year experience into a lifetime's sacrifice.

39 What if there is a crisis and I have to be evacuated from my post?

Peace Corps evacuations are very real occurrences, planned for by the PC administration and touched on during training. Some areas of the world are more prone to events leading to evacuations than others. Political instability, civil unrest, military coups, widespread corruption, rigged elections, suppression of the media, economic crises, invasion by outside forces, territorial disputes, cultural clashes, and a host of other problems can, independently or combined, erupt into violence and threaten the security of Peace Corps volunteers working in affected areas. Although the Peace Corps generally tries to limit its programs to countries that are socially, politically, and economically stable, often such occurrences arise without much warning and escalate rather quickly.

If you are unfortunate enough to get caught up in a situation that requires emergency action, you will receive instructions from the Peace Corps via communication channels established when you first arrive at your post. Options range from self-imposed "house arrest" (wait in your house until things in your town or village cool down) to evacuation from your country of service. In the event that you are evacuated, the Peace Corps will arrange for your transportation to the capital city, if necessary.

I witnessed only one evacuation while I was in the Peace Corps, which occurred when civil war threatened volunteers in a neighboring country. PCVs were evacuated to Cameroon, where they stayed until the Peace Corps decided on an appropriate next step. Some ended up transferring into my program and serving their remaining time in Cameroon; others opted to early COS or administratively separate and return to the States. No one was harmed during the evacuation, but all were affected by the violence and destruction they had witnessed before leaving. Fortunately, as I mentioned above, such occurrences are rare.

40 Do local police and government officials harass volunteers?

As with so many other aspects of Peace Corps life, it depends. In my village and region, police and "gendarmes" (army personnel) generally respected the Peace Corps, but were known to hassle volunteers traveling without their Peace Corps ID. This was especially true if the officials had been drinking on the job (which was not infrequent). In other countries, however, volunteers seldom have run-ins with the police or government soldiers and their encounters are usually cordial and friendly.

If you happen to be assigned to a country where local and national police have been known to harass volunteers or detain them in the hopes of procuring bribes, you'll be instructed during training on various ways to deal with the situation, and you'll be told who to turn to in the event that the situation gets ugly. In most cases, deferring to authority is usually a placating and effective strategy for bowing out of potentially confrontational situations. Other times, you may have to throw your weight around and threaten "embassy" or "headquarters" involvement if things feel like they are getting out of hand.

In most cases, as I mentioned above, officials who harass Peace Corps volunteers are looking for a bribe from the "rich Americans." If you speak a local language or can effectively explain what you are doing in the country, all the while refusing to provide a payoff and insisting that you are as poor as your neighbors, odds are they'll tire and eventually let you go. What I don't recommend is offering a bribe or paying an official if he threatens to jail you for whatever reason. Doing so sets a dangerous precedent for yourself and future volunteers by raising the hopes and expectations of corrupt officers, who may begin to see Peace Corps volunteers as ready sources of supplements to their incomes.

41 Is sexual harassment a problem for female volunteers?

Unfortunately, it can be. Women in most developing countries do not enjoy as much freedom, respect, or authority as women in developed countries do. They are often deprived of economic and political power, and denied rights that women in the West view as elementary. Conversely, in many developing countries, men dominate the power structure of state, business, community, and home. As such, female volunteers may be perceived and treated differently than their male counterparts by host country nationals. The export of U.S. pop culture—*Baywatch*, romance novels, MTV, fashion magazines, etc.—compounds the problem by portraying American women as promiscuous and sexually permissive. In Cameroon, French-dubbed American soap operas were a big hit via satellite television, as were sexually explicit Western films and pop icons/sex symbols like Madonna.

In general, the Peace Corps insists that volunteers be sensitive to the "effect their behavior has on their personal safety." They also maintain that the Peace Corps experience "almost always requires volunteers to change or limit some of their behaviors in deference to host country culture" (*Peace Corps Volunteer Handbook*, September 1995, p. 38). Despite volunteers' best efforts to minimize exposure to sexual harassment, however, situations may arise for which deference and sensitivity are decidedly inadequate responses. If you are verbally harassed, and you feel the attack is not rooted in cultural misunderstanding, by all means express your intolerance and proactively assert yourself. The prerogative is always yours to speak up when you feel harassed; you are only encouraged by the Peace Corps to think twice, since so many conflicts stem from misinterpretations and cultural differences.

Unwanted physical contact or sexual assault is another story. There is no instance when such behavior is justified, regardless of cultural divergences. In some countries, the Peace Corps encourages female volunteers to be aggressive and fight back when sexually assaulted, since a woman resisting a man is so uncommon it takes the aggressor by surprise. Many women PCVs carry pepper spray, whistles, or other items to alarm or disarm assailants. These items are often provided by Peace Corps or the security branch of the American embassies overseas. In Cameroon, the Peace Corps sponsored a two-day training course to teach all PCVs the basics of self-defense. Depending on where you serve, your Peace Corps training program may spend a considerable amount of time preparing volunteers to handle sexual harassment in the field.

If your physical security is ever threatened during your service, immediately inform your program and country directors. If the situation doesn't improve with time, most requests to be transferred to a different post are granted. In rare instances when volunteers are grievously assaulted, they are evacuated to the States for medical treatment and counseling.

As in the U.S., your best weapons are awareness and preparedness. When overseas, use common sense and heed the Peace Corps' advice on the subject, which will be tailored to your country of service. Don't compromise your values or safety, but realize that life in the Peace Corps may require a respect for cultural differences that may, at times, infuriate you. Most importantly, should you ever personally experience sexual assault or intolerable harassment, remember that you have the right to respond, react, and report the incident just as you would in the States.

Part VII
Staying in Touch
with Home

42 How will I receive mail in the Peace Corps?

Most Peace Corps posts are in remote locations in impoverished countries where the mail system is often rudimentary, unreliable, and anything but private. When you are halfway across the world, however, such a system somehow seems adequate. In the Peace Corps, even a three-month-old letter seems like a blessing, and a package that arrives with only half the contents pilfered by customs officials is like a Christmas gift from Santa himself.

That said, there are a few things you can do to help hasten and secure the passage and delivery of your mail. Have anyone sending you a care package scribble religious symbols and biblical quotes all over the outside of the box. This sounds silly, but it works. Though many of the countries in which Peace Corps serves are largely animist in religion, superstition runs high and even corrupt postal workers are wary of intercepting religious parcels. Along every step of the way, your mail will be subject to the whims of postal officials, customs officers, and delivery personnel who often take the liberty of rummaging through care packages in search of goodies from the U.S. If your mail is embellished with religious symbols, the odds of keeping it intact are improved. You may even want to ask the sender to write "Sister" or "Brother" before your name, to heighten the effect.

Another trick is to have your mail addressed to you in red ink. I've been told red ink is somewhat sacrosanct in many third world societies and is reserved for only the most official of letters and correspondences. Though I'm unsure about this explanation's validity, I can vouch for the trick's effectiveness, having seen several packages addressed in red ink delivered safely and expeditiously.

Before you leave the States, find out from the Peace Corps the address of your training site. That is where you'll be for your first three months overseas, so I recommend having friends and family start writing weeks before you leave the States if you want to get mail soon after you arrive. I didn't do that and consequently suffered through a grueling six-week period of mail silence before letters started trickling in. Once you know your village assignment, get a P.O. box at the closest post office as soon as possible. If you're posted to a bigger village or town, there may be a post office within walking distance of your house. If you're in a more remote location, you may have to take a bush taxi to the nearest big town to check your mail.

There is often an informal and effective system in the Peace Corps of having neighboring volunteers, who pass by or through your village, deliver mail to you on their way back from a mail run. Sometimes, if there is a cluster of volunteers who all get mail in the provincial capital or nearest big town, they will rent a P.O. box together and have copies of the key made. Other times there may be a Peace Corps rest house set up in a centrally located town, and any mail picked up from the local post office will get distributed to individual boxes in the Peace Corps house.

Picking up packages is a bit more complicated and can often turn into an entire afternoon's affair. You may receive a note from the post office declaring that they are in custody of a package addressed to you and indicating the official taxes and tariffs due to post bail and claim it. Notice I said "official." What they will not inscribe on the postal slip are the numerous unofficial bribes and gifts expected when you show up with your imploring look and desperate smile. They may double the declared fee; they may have you open your box in front of them and demand some of the contents (such as food items or magazines). In either case, I recommend that you stand firm and offer them nothing. Don't pay any bribes; don't give any gifts. It sets a bad precedent. If you loiter around and whine about the evils of corruption long enough, they'll tire of you and relinquish your package just to get you to leave.

Sending packages back home can also be tricky. Don't send items of value from your country of service to the States unless volunteers who have been there for a while have tried it and declared it to be safe. One PCV in my group insisted on sending all his film back home to be developed, rather than developing it in-country. He once sent a batch of five rolls, documenting his first three months at post, to his parents. They never received them, and he was devastated. Not every package you send from your country of service will disappear in transit. It will depend on where you serve and what you are sending (to a degree). But if you are burned even once, it will feel like once too many.

A surprising number of countries scattered throughout the developing world do have UPS offices in the larger cities. Though they will be reliable and insurable sources of mail transport, the cost of sending something back to the States via UPS is usually prohibitively high for Peace Corps volunteers.

Aside from packages, sending letters is relatively simple. No matter where you are, you should be able to get your hands on aerograms—that waxy, tissue-thin blue stationery that costs almost nothing to send, and allows you to squeeze in a couple of pages of text if you write small. Aerograms almost always find their way to their destination; it's just a question of how many detours and delays they encounter en route.

One sure way of transporting letters and packages both to and from the States is to have guests visiting Peace Corps volunteers act as couriers. If one of your fellow PCVs is expecting a visitor from the States, ask if you can arrange to have your family mail the visitor a letter or small package to be hand-carried to you. This assures quick and safe delivery. When that visitor is heading back to the States, ask if he or she minds carrying a few letters or a small pre-addressed and prestamped package to send to your friends or family. Burdensome as it may seem, you will assuredly be called on to return the favor one day when you have visitors from the States, so don't be shy.

Lastly, if you absolutely need something sent to you and wish to maximize the chances of it arriving in one piece, have it sent to the Peace Corps office rather than to your village or local post office. Eliminating the additional transport and handling required to deliver the package closer to you reduces the odds that an intermediary will steal it. The Peace Corps office is also a more "official" destination than your local post office, making it a less likely target for foul play. Once the office receives it, they'll send a note to your local P.O. box and you can pick it up the next time you're in town.

43

Will people be able to send me things through the embassy's diplomatic mail pouch?

Only if the items sent are work-related. Even so, you must ask your APCD or CD for approval. The diplomatic pouch is the embassy's tool for sending packages and letters back and forth from the States via the U.S. Postal Service. Pouches come and go with varying frequency, depending on the country, ranging anywhere from daily to weekly. The diplomatic pouch is exponentially safer than the local mail system for all the reasons I describe in Question 42.

Peace Corps volunteers are not granted access to the diplomatic pouch as a rule. However, if you need information for your project, tools available only in the States, documents or grant applications for planned work programs, and so on, you can request permission from your APCD or CD to use the pouch. In one instance, for example, a Peace Corps volunteer's work boots had worn out to the point where they were basically useless. He needed boots to visit farms and trek long distances to accomplish his work objectives, so he was granted permission to have a pair sent from REI in Seattle to the embassy via the diplomatic pouch. They arrived within weeks, which to those of us who had been sending and receiving packages all the while through the local postal system seemed nothing short of miraculous.

44 Can I get magazine subscriptions sent to me?

As I mentioned in Question 42, the mail system in many Peace Corps countries is anything but reliable. You can have subscriptions forwarded to your overseas address but don't count on receiving every issue. The ones that do arrive may be months old by the time you get them. What you'll need to do is call the magazine before you leave the States and give them the address of the Peace Corps office in the capital city. They may or may not require you to pay extra for postage. In some cases, they will forward the remainder of your subscription to the overseas address until it runs out without additional charges, but when you try to renew by mail they will ask for an extra twenty or thirty dollars to cover international shipping costs.

One of Peace Corps' surprise perks is a free subscription to *Newsweek* magazine. They come in bulk to the Peace Corps office and are distributed to volunteers' local mailboxes from there. They often get backlogged, skipping weeks here and there, then arriving in bundles of four or five, but they do provide a somewhat reliable source of information and entertainment over the course of two years.

Besides subscriptions, you can ask anyone sending you a care package to include a favorite magazine or two. You'd be surprised how entertaining and informative magazines can be when you have so much time to read and digest them. Without regular doses of CNN, MTV, or ESPN, magazines are one of the few sources of news that can keep you in touch with culture, politics, music, and sports in the States.

45 Will I be able to call the States?

Yes, you will be able to call home. The difficulty will be finding the nearest phone, figuring out the billing system, and making the extremely long-distance connection over often antiquated and inadequate phone lines. Some volunteers end up in countries where phones are in every town and village. Some may even have phones in their houses. For the most part, though, expect to be posted in a rural village with the nearest working phone a few hours away by bus or taxi.

Once you locate a phone, you'll probably have a few options for making the call home (or anywhere, for that matter). In many countries there are both public telephone booths and "teleboutiques." The former often require phone cards, which come in varying denominations ranging anywhere from the equivalent of one to ten dollars. They work much like the prepaid phone cards you can purchase here in the States. Their value is encoded on a magnetic strip on the back of the card, and once you insert it into the pay phone and connect with whomever you are calling, a digital meter will start counting down until the value reaches zero, at which point you are disconnected. You can buy phone cards at post offices and local stores—though if you buy them from private vendors, be wary of counterfeits or cards that have already been used.

Teleboutiques are often the preferred way to call home, especially if you frequent the same one and get to know the owner. They are small, privately run businesses that specialize in charging people to make and receive calls and faxes. Often there will be a private booth or two, with a phone connected to a meter. You make the call, then pay the owner for the units used, as indicated by the meter. Be sure to ask and agree on the per-unit charge before you make the call or, like with so many transactions between Peace Corps volunteers and local businesses, you'll lose your shirt.

In either case, teleboutique or pay phone, you may or may not be able to use an AT&T or Sprint-type calling card. It just depends on the service area of your provider. Before you head overseas, check with your calling card company to see if they have an access code for the country you'll be traveling to. If they do, it will be much less expensive than dialing direct and you'll be able to make the call with the assistance of an English-speaking operator. If they don't, don't worry, there are still tricks to help you call home cheaply.

Regardless of whether you call from a pay phone or a teleboutique, the best way to save money is to arrange for a "call-back." Since calling the States from a foreign country is often three or four times more expensive than calling that same country from the States, it makes sense to have someone at home call you. Most volunteers will go to a pay phone or teleboutique, dial home, connect with a voice on the other end, and speak as fast as they can to relay the fact that: a) they are alive and healthy, b) they are at a working phone and will be there for the next few minutes, and c) the person they want to speak with should call them back immediately. Then they slam the phone down and find out how much those three precious minutes cost them. In Cameroon it was between six and ten dollars, depending on where I called from and the exact amount of time I took.

Then you sit and wait, and hope that whoever is trying to call you back has luck with the international phone lines. The lines are often busy, and receiving the call-back may take ten to fifteen minutes, or it may not come at all. In the meantime, you have to rabidly fend off other customers who need to use the phone, lest they tie up the line on your end.

When you do receive the call-back, you will not be charged if you are at a pay phone (just as you would not be charged to receive a call at a pay phone in the States). If you are at a teleboutique, you may have to pay a small fee for tying up the line, but I encourage you to try to strike a deal with the owner. Tell him or her that if you are allowed to receive calls from the States free of charge, you will always make your long-distance calls there, and you will recommend the teleboutique to all of your Peace Corps friends in the region.

With regard to arranging call-backs, there is a Peace Corps trick to minimize phone charges. Oftentimes volunteers will get together and start a phone chain to the States. For example, say Warren calls home and speaks with his mom for a while. At the end of their conversation, Warren will ask his mom to call Amy's folks and let them know that she is there, at the same number, waiting for a call. Once Amy's parents call and speak with her for a while, she will ask them to pass a message on to Jeremy's parents, letting them know that he is waiting for a call, and so on. Though this kind of phone chain may sound extreme to save yourself a few dollars every month or so, once you adjust to the local economy and realize just how much money six to ten dollars is in most developing countries, you'll understand why it's an efficient and worthwhile strategy.

As I mentioned in Question 42, several Peace Corps programs have established regional rest houses in provincial capitals or towns which are accessible to clusters of volunteers. These houses usually provide lodging for folks that come to town to shop, bank, hang out, call home, recover from illness, or whatever. Many of these houses also have phones that can't dial out, but can receive calls. Volunteers with access to such phones often call home from a nearby pay phone, but arrange to have the other party call them at the rest house, where they can hold conversations in a more relaxed and private environment. Calling home in the Peace Corps is a real treat; you'll want to do all you can to make it easy to connect and communicate.

46 Will I have e-mail access?

As I'm sure you know, e-mail is a great way to stay in touch with friends and family, and gather information to help you with various projects. It is, however, still far beyond the level of technology found in most parts of the world. The *1997 Peace Corps Volunteer Survey Report* states, "Only 7% of all respondents always had access to e-mail, another 8% sometimes had access, and 85% never had access. . . . Access to e-mail was concentrated in ECAM (Europe/ Central Asia/Mediterranean) where 40% had access at least sometimes compared with only 5% in Africa" (Peace Corps Office of Planning, Policy and Analysis, Oct. 1, 1997, p. 26). E-mail capability requires phone lines, computers, servers, and skilled programmers and engineers. As such, your access to e-mail services in the Peace Corps will depend on which region of the world, which country, and which post you are assigned to.

As indicated above, many Eastern European countries are hooked into the Internet and have e-mail capability. Volunteers sent to Eastern Europe are also more likely to be placed in bigger towns or cities, increasing the chances that they will have access to e-mail. In most other developing regions of the world, however, chances are slim that you will have e-mail readily available, unless the country itself is fairly modernized or you are posted in the capital city. If you are sent to Africa, Latin America, or parts of Asia, you will probably only run into e-mail at the Peace Corps office in the capital. Even that is no guarantee. If there is e-mail access in the Peace Corps office, you will most likely be able to send and receive messages there while you are in town. But since you may only come into the office once or twice every quarter, it won't be a regular means of communication or information exchange.

Part VIII
The Social Scene

47 How close will I live to another volunteer?

In many Peace Corps countries, several volunteers are assigned to the same village. In others, you may be a short trip away from your nearest neighbor. It's rare to be so isolated that you won't at least have the option of visiting a fellow volunteer if you want or need to. Overall, the Peace Corps tries to cluster volunteers close together in an effort to create a support network that benefits the volunteer and the program by fostering happier, more productive workers. As reported in the *1997 Peace Corps Volunteer Survey Report*, "most respondents lived near other PCVs—70% lived an hour or less from other PCVs, 24% lived two to four hours away, 4% five to ten hours away, 1% ten to twenty-four hours away, and less than 1% lived more than twenty-four hours away" (Peace Corps Office of Planning, Policy and Analysis, Oct. 1, 1997, p. 16).

In cases where the Peace Corps places more than one volunteer in a village or town, often the volunteers aren't in the same program. One may be doing forestry, one could be a health volunteer, and another could be doing community development. With folks who were clustered with volunteers, it was a crapshoot as to whether they all got along or ended up avoiding each other. Individual personalities will play a big role in determining your interactions. One thing to keep in mind if you are assigned a post-mate or two, however, is that there is a danger in relying too heavily on him/her/them for company and support, thereby delaying or inhibiting the process of acculturation and adjustment. The temptation of having someone right there with whom you can speak English, talk about familiar things, listen to familiar music, and create a detached environment from your foreign and intimidating surroundings may be powerful. But for those who do strike a balance and successfully cultivate village friendships, colleagues, and interests, it can be a tremendous comfort to have a friend and fellow volunteer with whom to share so many experiences.

When the Peace Corps puts just one volunteer in each village, each will most likely find that they are within a few hours' journey of the nearest volunteer. That journey may be by bike, bus, train, foot, or car, and may take two hours or eight hours, but it will be comforting to know that you can reach someone familiar (culturally speaking) within a day if the need arises. And it probably will. In my case, the closest volunteer was about two hours north of me. We got together at least twice a month to cook spaghetti dinners, listen to music, play cribbage, go for hikes, talk about our experiences and anxieties, attend social functions in the village, share work experiences, and plan vacations and trips. There were times when I visited that person because I wanted to, and times when I did so because I needed to. Make use of your fellow volunteers when you're overseas; they will help make the experience both easier and more memorable.

48 How often will I see other volunteers?

It goes without saying that if you have post-mates, you will have substantially greater opportunities to see other volunteers than if you don't. That said, the amount of interaction you have with other volunteers once you are assigned to your village is really up to you. There will probably be times when you feel like you need to see a fellow volunteer. Perhaps you'll be looking for someone to whom you can vent in "American English" when you encounter frustrations in your village; or you may want to share a great cultural experience with someone who understands the magnitude and importance of that event without explanation. When you're feeling down or homesick, you may want the company of someone who can commiserate with you. Or you may want someone you can invite to share in a village ceremony, someone with whom you can relive that moment later in life. There will also be times when you get sick and want someone to lean on who has been there and knows what it's like. In essence, there will most likely be times when you'll feel compelled to seek out familiar ground and the comforting presence of a fellow volunteer.

Aside from those times, however, it really is up to you. Whether you intend to stay put in your village or town and avoid Peace Corps parties, trips, and functions, or you decide to participate fully in every Peace Corps event throughout the two years, is your call. There will be parties at people's posts and in centralized locations where people can meet up easily. There will be vacations and trips (officially sanctioned and clandestine) to take. There will be numerous opportunities to participate in official committees, training courses, ceremonies, and administrative volunteer groups that revolve around the Peace Corps office in the capital. I knew volunteers who avoided all that jazz and left their villages only when absolutely necessary, and others who divided their time among their village, their Peace Corps friends, and their commitments to Peace Corps' "extracurricular" committees and planning groups.

Your experience will be what you make of it, and your interactions with other volunteers in relation to the time spent in your village can make a difference. As with most other aspects of Peace Corps life where you will face choices and decisions that have an impact, my advice is to try to strike a balance. I found it important to maintain ties and friendships with my Peace Corps colleagues, and many of those friendships will, I hope, endure long into the future. I also fostered meaningful and enriching friendships in my village, without which I wouldn't have been able to work and live so far from home for two years. Though you may feel pressure from the Peace Corps administration to stay at your post and minimize your interactions with other volunteers, and you may feel pressure from your Peace Corps friends to maximize interactions with them at the expense of your life in the village, have in mind the way you want your experience to be and strive to attain it.

49

What is the drug and alcohol situation like?

Many who join the Peace Corps are shocked to discover how prevalent drug and alcohol use is within the volunteer community. Pressure to drink or smoke often bombards volunteers from several angles. Drugs and alcohol may be cheap, abundant, and freely consumed by fellow volunteers during social events. Within a volunteer's village, local customs and traditions may revolve around shared drinking experiences (i.e., imbibing freshly tapped palm wine or recently fermented corn beer). Inevitable periods of boredom or depression at post may prompt volunteers to use alcohol or drugs as a means of "escape."

The Peace Corps addresses this topic only briefly during training. They admonish volunteers against succumbing to pressure from peers, counterparts, or their village environments. The fact is, in some countries and Peace Corps programs, to drink in your village or do drugs with other volunteers presents itself as a quick and effective way to acculturate or gain acceptance at a time in your life when "fitting in" has never before meant so much. As a way of dealing with boredom or loneliness at post, drugs and alcohol are attractive alternatives for many. If you aren't aware of the dangers associated with approaching cultural and social immersion from that angle, or if you fail to see the pitfalls in avoiding or creatively coping with moments of boredom and inactivity in your village, it can be a disaster. Aside from the negative health and psychological effects associated with drug and alcohol use, volunteers under the influence may compromise their safety and security by engaging in high-risk activities, such as practicing unsafe sex or instigating fights.

What can you do? Be aware that, especially during your first few months in training and at post, you will be psychologically vulnerable and eager to adapt to your new environment. Be aware that drinking or doing drugs may seem to be a real door-opener for gaining acceptance from your peers and from the people in your village. Be aware that some volunteers go overboard and come to rely on alcohol or drugs to get them through their whole two years.

Be aware of any severe changes in your drinking or drug use patterns, and use the Peace Corps medical office for counseling or assistance if you suspect you have (or are developing) a problem. Make a list of things to do at post when you are bored or have time to kill (cooking, fixing your bike, reading, writing letters, learning to play the harmonica, updating your journal, taking pictures, hiking and exploring, visiting friends, etc.). And don't forget who you are; it's good to bend once in a while to experience something new, but be careful not to break.

50 What is the dating scene like in the Peace Corps?

It is alive and kicking. Peace Corps volunteers date other Peace Corps volunteers all the time. And the reasons are fairly obvious. You have a small number of people with certain common interests and goals, living far from home and sharing intense life experiences for two years. In that kind of environment, it doesn't take long for friendships to blossom into intimate relationships. Some of those intimate relationships last only a night; others end up lasting a lifetime.

Although at first you may look around at your fellow trainees and marvel at how different everyone seems from yourself, soon after arriving in-country you'll transcend those differences and see that there is, indeed, a common thread that connects most volunteers. As you begin to rely on your friendships with others to help make training more manageable and meaningful, you also begin to see how easy it is for "closer" relationships to form.

In addition to environmental and personality factors, there is also the hormonal factor. Most Peace Corps volunteers are young adults with active hormones; as they initially grapple with the social and cultural isolation imposed on them by their foreign surroundings, their hormones offer a simple solution: cling to each other like Velcro. Inter-volunteer hook-ups don't always end after training, either. Peace Corps parties, extended visits from other volunteers, and other gatherings (formal and informal) over the two years offer numerous opportunities to strike up a romance or two.

For as long as the Peace Corps has existed, volunteers have also had intimate relationships with host country nationals. Just as sure as someone in your training group will eventually date another volunteer, someone else will date an HCN before the two years are up. Officially, the Peace Corps doesn't say much on this topic. They focus instead on encouraging safe sex, regardless of who your partner is. In parts of the world where AIDS and STDs are rampant, dating HCNs can be risky business. In fact, during training we were shown a video in which five AIDS-infected former PCVs were interviewed, all of whom had contracted the disease through sex with an HCN (refer to Question 38).

Aside from the health aspect, keep in mind your professional obligations to the Peace Corps and make sure personal relationships don't compromise them. If you're attracted to the chief's daughter, for example, but you know that a failed relationship with her would put you on the village's "most wanted" list, think twice before striking up a romance. A volunteer in my group alienated himself from his local community by dating a woman who flaunted their relationship to her peers. Other villagers became jealous of her and spiteful toward him, to the point where it substantially impeded his efforts to accomplish project-related goals. Peace Corps ended up transferring him to another village in a different part of the country (his girlfriend went with him). It seemed to be an administrative headache, though they were both happy in the end.

One aspect of Peace Corps dating that you may find grossly unappealing, incidentally, is the associated gossip network. As with a tiny college or a small firm here in the States, word travels quickly among friends and colleagues. You may think you've begun a clandestine relationship with your neighbor or the volunteer three villages away, but rest assured the Peace Corps grapevine will transmit that information to the far reaches of the country before you can bat an eye. Phone lines may not exist, the mail system may be primeval, and volunteers may be separated by vast distances—but gossip in the Peace Corps makes the Internet look low-tech. Of course, as with any grapevine, the information about volunteers that races around the country is rarely accurate or reliable. But to a group of people hungry for entertainment and amusement, it serves a purpose and knows no mercy, so be forewarned as you contemplate wooing whomever you may have your eye on.

51 What happens if I want to marry a host country national?

When you spend two years in a small community, getting to know local customs, languages, traditions, and people, opportunities arise to meet special people and form close relationships that may grow into lifelong commitments. The Peace Corps does not officially support or discourage such relationships; they only insist that you meet your obligations to the organization and keep personal issues from compromising your programmatic responsibilities. The Peace Corps' sole requirement concerning volunteer marriages to HCNs is that the CD be informed.

I attended a number of weddings between PCVs and HCNs while I was in-country. They were joyous occasions, attended by relatives of the bride and groom, fellow volunteers, Peace Corps staff, and local friends. In most cases, the newlyweds flew to the States after the PCV finished his/her service to begin a new life together. Though there are no statistics on success or divorce rates resulting from Peace Corps marriages to HCNs, the couples I knew seemed well matched and happy, impressing me with the unpredictable and powerful ways the Peace Corps may impact one's life.

Part IX
The Toughest Job You'll Ever Love?

52 What is the work schedule like?

It depends on your program. Education volunteers are tied to their school's schedules, working during school terms and vacationing during holidays and term breaks. Health volunteers working at clinics may be expected to put in full days in accordance with agreements worked out with the clinic administrator. Agriculture and forestry volunteers tailor their work schedules to accommodate the seasons, the farmers' schedules, crop rotations, and so on.

In my case, I tended to spend around two or three hours per day, four days per week with individual farmers practicing hands-on agroforestry. I spent another few hours each week providing demonstrations or "extension" (training seminars) to groups of farmers. The rest of my time was divided among secondary projects, socializing (which is, as your trainers will tell you, part of your job), and doing my own thing.

In truth, you will have a great deal of independence and flexibility when setting your schedule, so a lot will rest on your initiative and willingness to work. Some volunteers work hard. They put in long days on the farm, they tutor students over the holidays, they work weekends at the local clinic. Others aren't so motivated. As long as you are accomplishing your project goals and being productive at post, the Peace Corps administration won't breathe down your neck. Just take care not to abuse the independence—there have been cases in which wayward volunteers were sent packing due to insufficient work-related progress at post.

During training, you'll be told that Peace Corps is a twenty-four-hour-a-day, seven-day-a-week job. To a degree that is true. When you are at your post, the line between work and leisure can often be thin. Socializing with farmers or fellow teachers is as important to developing effective working relationships as meeting them on the farm or at school. Attending community celebrations or local ceremonies may do more for promoting your projects than months of field work and demonstrations. In the Peace Corps, your identity is so closely tied to your organization and its objectives, it's hard not to see links between your social activities and your "official" responsibilities.

53 How much supervision is there for volunteers in the field?

Not a lot. Once you get to your village, you have a degree of independence that few other jobs offer. You can be as proactive or inactive as you want. You have the opportunity and authority to design, implement, manage, and monitor entire programs with little, if any, intervention from the Peace Corps office. They are there to guide you, and serve as a technical resource if you need them, but they will not be managing your work while you are in the field.

Your APCD will try to visit your post at least once every six months. That's four times during your entire two years. As such, your day-to-day schedule, and your overall work-related accomplishments will depend on your initiative and level of motivation (refer to Question 52). There may be a Peace Corps volunteer leader (PCVL) nearby to help you with technical difficulties you encounter, but even that individual will not be "supervising" you in the traditional sense of the word.

My advice is to take advantage of the opportunity to gain invaluable project experience, and develop useful self-management skills. Remind yourself that, in your next job, you may find yourself clinging to a corporate ladder, struggling for years just to climb to the next rung. In the Peace Corps there is no ladder. Volunteers work independently at post and are empowered to start secondary projects, apply for grants, do public outreach and education, evaluate project successes, and much more.

At the same time, take advantage of the independence to meet personal goals. Travel, visit friends, see the country, relax, and enjoy life as only a freewheelin' PCV can. Too many Peace Corps volunteers get so locked into their work and projects at post, their two years pass them by before they realize how little of the country they've seen, and how much of the culture remains unexplored. Be social, participate in Peace Corps committees and training opportunities, throw parties, have visitors, and take vacations. Find the balance point between work and play where you feel comfortable, and stay there.

54

Will I work with other international development agencies while I'm overseas?

You may. There are numerous development agencies operating overseas and, depending on where you serve, you may encounter one or several of them at your post. They may be working on projects that overlap with your program; they may be focusing on completely separate issues. They may maintain a staff of twenty people, complete with Land Rovers and computers; they may consist of one guy and his notepad. They may welcome you and invite you to collaborate; they may have a disdain for Peace Corps volunteers or feel protective of their projects.

The Peace Corps does not discourage volunteers from collaborating with other development agencies, provided that the work is relevant to the volunteers' primary or secondary projects and doesn't usurp all of their time. If you find a nongovernmental organization (NGO) to collaborate with, take care to avoid becoming "free labor" by overextending yourself, and avoid the appearance of working for it rather than for the Peace Corps.

You should also be aware of the NGO's reputation in your work area before you agree to collaborate. It may be that its approach toward development is more top-down and resource-intensive than grassroots and labor-intensive. If so, people in your town or village may perceive the organization as an elitist outsider that imposes development rather than encourages it.

If you do manage to find a group that seems worthy of collaboration, and they are amenable to the idea, consider it a good opportunity to enrich your Peace Corps experience. Working together will assuredly multiply the impact of your efforts, while exposing you to professional contacts and experiences that could prove valuable even after your service with the Peace Corps is over. You'll undoubtedly learn more about development, learn more about NGO administration, and discover new techniques to accomplish project goals. Similarly, it boosts the Peace Corps' exposure to sister agencies and encourages cooperation between PCVs and NGOs in the future.

55 Is the Peace Corps effective as a development agency?

Here's a whole can of worms that, if opened, could fill the pages of a book by itself. So let me just puncture the can a little and let a few worms wiggle out. Does the Peace Corps work? Does it accomplish its aims? Does it effect positive change at the grassroots level? In some respects, yes; in others, not really. When I was there, serving my two years overseas, I thought it almost ludicrous to imagine that my efforts mattered to anyone but myself. I had little faith in my work as effecting lasting, positive change on my village, much less the country of Cameroon. I felt my own ambitions and goals were being fulfilled for the most part, while the greater goals of "development" and "intercultural exchange" consisted mostly of administrative rhetoric.

Of course, those were impressions from the field, amid daily struggles with the basics of life in a developing country. It's hard to think objectively about the "big picture" when you're living in a small, relatively isolated corner of the world. Now that I'm back and have had time to reflect on the entire experience, I see my life in Cameroon as having impacted the people with whom I lived and worked in a much broader and more definable way.

It's true—no volunteer is going to leave his or her post having single-handedly saved a rain forest or boosted a nation's economy. No volunteer will COS having reversed national trends in infant mortality. No volunteer will be able to claim they succeeded in dispelling all the myths and stereotypes about Americans in their villages. But each volunteer should be able to look back at their Peace Corps experience and put their finger on a few lives they helped better and minds they helped broaden. When they do that, they will realize the enormity of their accomplishments and the impressive effect those changes have on a larger scale.

Peace Corps volunteers have a tough mission to begin with; they are charged with the onerous duty of effecting progress and development at the grassroots level in parts of the world most resistant to change. They must promote intercultural exchange and introduce new methods of tackling important social and environmental issues, often in societies rooted to ancient traditions, religions, and superstitions. They are deprived of the material and monetary means that other development agencies rely upon to force that change, and are left only with technical knowledge and an elemental ability to inspire change through collaboration and education. Given such formidable hurdles in accomplishing the agency's goals, it's no wonder so many PCVs question their contribution to "development" in the academic sense of the word. For most, development emerges as a tangent to the everyday relationships and experiences of village life.

Ideally, Peace Corps volunteers integrate so well into their communities that they are able to work creatively from the inside out. They make friends with their colleagues, they make use of available resources, they rely on cultural exchange and dialogue to bridge technical and resource gaps. Such an approach inevitably produces a more sustainable and widespread change, though, from the field, volunteers rarely have the vantage point to appreciate it. Although the agency's goals are not always met by each volunteer and program, a testament to the organization's overall impact is the demand for volunteers by host country governments and the widespread (bipartisan) approval of the Peace Corps here in the United States.

56

What are some common criticisms of the Peace Corps?

While, on the whole, the Peace Corps is viewed as an important federal institution worthy of its budget and directive, there are those who argue for funding cutbacks and organizational changes. Similarly, although most would characterize PCVs as exemplary citizens making tremendous sacrifices for noble causes, others question volunteers' motives and doubt their contributions.

The harshest criticisms of the Peace Corps often come from PCVs or RPCVs themselves, stemming from their direct exposure to critical aspects of the organization and its services. Their comments run the gamut—from arguing that the Peace Corps experience is too long, to arguing that it isn't long enough; from petitioning for greater funding for grassroots projects, to lamenting the elevated status of volunteers in the village whose monthly stipends are deemed excessive. Many volunteers feel that the Peace Corps' training program should provide more technical guidance. Others call for less administrative and programmatic direction for volunteers in the field. Some are convinced that the Peace Corps' prime directive (and hidden agenda) is to serve U.S. foreign policy interests, to the detriment of its development efforts. Others, still, point to limitations that volunteer attrition and turnover have on sustainability. All of the above criticisms have merit and ring true to an extent. If you flip forward to Question 73, though, you may get a sense of how quickly those sentiments soften with time.

Critics outside of the Peace Corps' family circle largely target volunteers' motives and the agency's capability to effect lasting change. The stereotype of PCVs as hippie throwbacks with too much free time on their hands is sometimes embraced by these detractors. They not only pigeonhole the volunteer experience as yet another thrill for Gen Xers, but wonder what contributions to third world development a twenty-two-year-old fine arts major can truly make. They point to the failures of relatively affluent development agencies such as the World Bank, the U.S. Agency for International Development (USAID), or the United Nations Development Program (UNDP) and wonder how, in comparison, a nickel-and-dime operation like the Peace Corps can combat issues of global importance. Lastly, critics insist that Peace Corps volunteers themselves are the prime beneficiaries of their service abroad. For PCVs, they argue, the experience is an opportunity to learn another language, see some of the world, and enrich their personal world view, all on the taxpayers' bill. For HCNs, they say, it provides a succession of random Americans intruding on their culture, living off of their generosity, and leaving once the novelty wears off.

As you consider joining, factor in the Peace Corps' criticisms, but keep in mind that the organization is generally praised for its persistence in educating and helping the world, one person at a time. As I mention in Question 70, no matter what you learn about the Peace Corps during your two years—its ups and downs, its bright spots and blemishes—you'll quickly realize that most people in the States have a much simpler, more noble impression of the organization. No development agency is flawless, but the Peace Corps' reputation and longevity attest to its overall success.

Part X
Rules to Live By—
Peace Corps Policy

57 Will I be able to have friends and family visit from the States?

Yes, and I highly recommend you do so. You will possess a thorough knowledge of the language, culture, and geography of your country of service, and will therefore be able to show them around like few others can. As expensive as the round-trip ticket may be, once they get there they will pay virtually nothing for food or lodging. You will have a network of Peace Corps friends scattered throughout the country with whom you'll be able to stay and use as a travel resource. You'll be "up" on which food is good, which is bad, which is cheap, and which is a real treat. You'll be able to bargain for them in the local language to secure deals on souvenirs and gifts. You'll know how to travel like locals—on bush taxis, trains, buses—which, in and of itself, is half the adventure and fun. And the list goes on. . . .

Now the technicalities: you are not supposed to take vacation days during your first three months at post (see Question 66). This means, unless you plan on leaving your visitors behind while you go to work everyday, it isn't practical to invite people to visit then. The rest of your service is fair game. Have as many people as you want come visit (within reason), and have them stay for *at least* three to five weeks to make it worth their (and your) time.

Well before the trip, have your visitor get in touch with the embassy of your country in Washington, D.C., to find out how to get a visa and how much it will cost. Some countries will require a written invitation from you before issuing a tourist visa to your guests. Also, if your guests need malaria prophylaxis, have them contact their health care provider to see if it's covered through insurance.

It's often helpful to spend half an hour brainstorming a realistic packing list to send to visitors before their trip. Keep in mind the seasons, the places you plan on taking them, and their baggage weight limitations. Use the opportunity to have them bring you goodies, too. There's nothing like a box of Reese's Cups or a package of new cotton underwear to recharge you after months of eating okra stew and watching your boxers or bras disintegrate from hundreds of hand-scrubbing washes.

You may also want to ask your visitors to reserve space in their luggage for care packages and small gifts from families of fellow volunteers. As I mention in Question 42, packages sent through international and local mail systems often break or disappear. It's nice if families of volunteers can rest assured that their mail will reach its destination quickly and intact. You may want the favor returned later, too.

Although it's great to have lots of visitors, and it breaks up the time nicely, keep in mind that you don't want to spend the entire two years entertaining guests and playing tour guide. Don't laugh, I know a few people who had friends and relatives from the States coming through like commuters at rush hour. When that happens, not only do you start feeling alienated from your village and work, but you also start resenting your guests and feeling that your Peace Corps experience is being compromised.

58 How often do volunteers quit before their two years are over?

More often than you may think. The Peace Corps average is thirty-three percent. In other words, on your first day of training, look around the room and expect that fully one-third of your group will not be attending the COS conference two years down the road. People quit early for all kinds of reasons, none of which is invalid or trivial. Making that decision is often painful and traumatic. Although the Peace Corps doesn't encourage it, they don't discourage it either. The door to home is always left open, which can be both comforting and distracting at the same time.

Leaving early in Peace Corps jargon is called "early terminating," or "ET'ing" for short. Volunteers ET for reasons as distinct and different as the individuals themselves. Some leave because they miss their boyfriends or girlfriends. Some leave because they realize they'd rather be in graduate school. Some leave because they have the misfortune of falling sick a lot and tire of worrying about their health for two years. Some leave because they discover they aren't interested in their Peace Corps program and can't fathom digging wells or weighing babies month after month. Others don't like the climate, don't like the food, don't like the music . . . who knows? Inevitably, though, you'll see a few of your fellow trainees head back home before training is over. Others will follow at various points during the two years.

People ET in waves. The first group typically leaves during training, having decided that the prospect of living and working overseas for two years is unbearable, or at least vastly different from their expectations. The second wave hits between three and six months after training—far and away the most trying and difficult period of the Peace Corps. Many refer to that period as the "make it or break it" months. After three to six months, you've either established a work load, learned more of the language, acclimated to solo living (washing clothes, hauling water, cooking food), and made friends in the village, or you haven't. If you haven't, you'll likely conclude that your lifestyle is unsustainable and you'll feel the pressure to leave.

The third and final wave hits around the one-year mark. People who ET after a year usually do so for professional or programmatic reasons. Perhaps they find their Peace Corps work unsatisfying. Perhaps their work is nonexistent and they feel they are biding their time. Perhaps they hear from graduate schools and don't want to defer admission for a year. Perhaps they feel their villages aren't a good fit for their personalities and they don't want to go through the ordeal of transferring villages and starting all over again.

Whatever the case, more people than you think ET and you can't predict who those people will be. Some of the most upbeat and optimistic trainees and volunteers may bail after a few weeks or months. Some of the most pessimistic and bitter volunteers may stay for the whole two years. It's best to withhold judgment about people that ET, especially since you may wake up one day and find that you are one of them. Just about everyone I knew seriously considered ET'ing at least once during their service. When you find yourself thinking that everything stinks—your job, your village, your life, your health, your mental attitude, your emotional state, your house, your colleagues, your program, and your country— ET'ing can look like a nice ticket to paradise. It's up to you to discourage yourself, so think hard about what you're experiencing and use your friends and family to help sort it out before jumping through a hoop that you can't go back through. If you still want to ET—go for it. No one knows what's best for you but you.

On a personal note, I should say that most (if not all) of the volunteers I knew who ET'd later came to regret it. I say this only because it struck me, when talking to these folks, how much they wished they had stuck through the two years. It wasn't until most of them reached the States that they realized life back here isn't a bed of roses, either. They ended up missing friends they'd made in the Peace Corps, the diversity of culture and life in the village, and the exotic and sometimes surreal environments of the countries they'd left. As with everything else in life, things usually get better if you give them time. A good general rule to live by if you feel like you really want to ET is to wait a couple of weeks and see how you feel then. The option is always there—right up until the day before you officially COS. You may as well wait a while to see if things shape up or problems resolve themselves before leaving. With family emergencies and grad school acceptances, you may not have the luxury of giving yourself some time to think things over carefully. But in most other instances, I'd advise patience and processing before packing.

---

59 What is the procedure for quitting early?

The Peace Corps' attitude toward volunteers who want to ET is pretty straightforward. They know that if you are unhappy, for whatever reason, you should probably go home. They may ask you once if you're sure; they may not even do that. They don't want to momentarily talk you out of leaving, only to have you to return to your village, sulk for a few more weeks, then decide to ET again. So if you come into the office to announce your decision to ET, don't do it with the hopes that your APCD will try to dissuade you.

The actual process is relatively simple. Once you announce your intent to ET, you'll go through a quick series of "exit interviews" with your APCD and CD. You'll tell them why you have decided to leave early and how you reached your decision. They'll be interested to know if your village played a factor (did your neighbors stone you every morning?), if your program played a factor (were you supposed to be teaching English in a village where the only school burned down three years ago?), or if it was something else that could be rectified by transferring you to another village or working through the problem. Keep in mind that transferring villages is no easy feat, however, and if you haven't previously approached the Peace Corps administration about moving to another post they may not believe that "dissatisfaction with work and village" lies at the root of the problem. They'll be more likely to conclude that you simply aren't happy in the Peace Corps, and will accept your decision to ET without resistance. They will also be trying to decide if your post should be replaced with another volunteer once you leave or abandoned by the Peace Corps altogether, so be careful what you say. It'll be easy to blame your village for all your woes and troubles, but think twice before pointing any fingers—you may cheat your village out of help they need, and a future volunteer out of a great experience.

Before you leave for the States, you'll need to submit to Peace Corps' COS medical examination, a thorough "systems-check" designed to test for amoebas, viruses, worms, HIV, schisto, filaria, and any other diseases common to the area. The exam will take approximately two to three days. If you haven't already lugged your belongings into the office, you should get a day or two to return to your village and pack up.

When you ET, you will receive your readjustment allowance totaling $225 for every month you were in-country, including training. You will not be given the cash-in-lieu-of-ticket option discussed in Question 67. The Peace Corps will purchase your return ticket to the States and you must follow the itinerary without deviation (unless you shell out your own cash to change it). In other words, you can't really ET and use the return ticket to hang out in Europe for a while or travel to Nepal. Depending on how long you served before ET'ing, and the reasons you cited for leaving early, you may still get noncompetitive eligibility for jobs in the federal government when you get back to the States (see Question 71).

As the Peace Corps states in their volunteer handbook, resignations are final and may not be reconsidered or appealed. In other words, before setting the wheels in motion, make sure your decision is final and is the right one for you.

60 Can I get kicked out of the Peace Corps?

There are several "Golden Rules" in Peace Corps which, if violated, can earn you a one-way ticket home. They differ from country to country, but often include these (in no particular order):

1. Driving or riding a motorcycle without a helmet (or in some countries, driving or riding a motorcycle at all)

2. Failing to take any required medications (including malaria prophylaxes)

3. Crossing an international border without notifying the Peace Corps

4. Using, or being accused of using, illicit drugs

5. Entering "restricted zones"—areas determined by the Peace Corps (and usually the U.S. embassy) to be dangerous for one reason or another

6. Accepting money for services rendered during your Peace Corps experience

7. Involving yourself in local or national politics overseas (i.e., participating in rallies, protests, demonstrations, etc.)

Of course, nothing is ever as simple as it seems. In order to be kicked out for the above sins, you have to be caught. I'm not trying to sound devious, but you should be aware that volunteers do violate these rules in certain circumstances and get away with it, if they use common sense.

For example, Peace Corps volunteers in countries around the world often encounter cheap and plentiful supplies of marijuana. Using discretion and subtlety, they obtain and consume it without administrative repercussions. Others cross international borders surreptitiously to visit Peace Corps friends or purchase souvenirs without declaring official vacation days. Others, still, opt not to take their malaria prophylaxis due to adverse physical reactions and unwanted side effects. Though all of the above, if discovered, constitute grounds for instant termination, they are practiced routinely and privately, out of sight of the Peace Corps administration.

My advice is to avoid influences or activities that may compromise your reputation or standing with Peace Corps officials. There aren't many rules in the Peace Corps, but the ones that exist are not taken lightly when broken. If you decide to bend or break a rule, do so privately and discreetly. Be sure you fully understand the risks and possible consequences of your actions, and don't expect leniency if you're caught. The Peace Corps understands and respects your rights as an adult and an individual, but when it comes to upholding regulations designed to safeguard your health and well-being, they are unyielding.

61 How many volunteers extend their service beyond the first two years?

Lots. Volunteers extend for various reasons. Some initiate projects that take longer than two years to complete—projects they feel obliged to see through to the end. Some become emotionally attached to people in their villages and find it difficult to leave for personal reasons. Some relish the relatively structure-free and independent life that the Peace Corps provides. Some decide to apply for positions as Peace Corps volunteer leaders (PCVLs) or trainers for the next group of volunteers. A few fear the upheaval and difficult process of readjusting to life in the U.S. (refer to Question 69).

Extending for a third year, however, is more complicated than it may seem. There are a limited number of extension slots each year, dictated by the Peace Corps' budget and annual appropriation. If you wish to extend, you must formally apply and interview with your APCD. Volunteers most likely to be approved for extensions are those whose primary reasons are work or project related. Those who apply for personal reasons rarely receive top priority on the extension list.

As I mentioned above, some people extend in order to become PCVLs. PCVLs are third-year volunteers who act as intermediaries between other volunteers in their program and their APCD. They live in a provincial capital or big town, giving them access to a cluster of volunteers. They provide personal and programmatic support by visiting volunteers in the field and helping them with technical or site-specific problems. They often live in more modern houses with electricity and phones, enabling them to contact the Peace Corps office regularly. They work closely with APCDs to coordinate meetings, conferences, and site visits, and are given a limited supervisory role over their volunteer peers.

If you decide to extend for a third year to be a PCVL, ask your APCD how and when to apply. The process can be highly competitive, as usually only the most motivated, committed, and productive volunteers express interest. You must complete a written application and interview with your APCD. Not all PCVLs love their job, so talk to your PCVL before you apply to gain some insight into the position and to help you decide if it's right for you.

If you extend, you'll be entitled to a four-week homeleave trip between your second and third years. The Peace Corps will provide you with a round-trip ticket to the States and will pay you a modest per diem. If you don't want to visit the States, you can take the air-fare money and buy a ticket for another destination. I knew one volunteer who spent his homeleave in London, visiting his girlfriend. His family wasn't pleased, but the option was there for him to exercise.

If you ET during your third year, you are liable for the costs of the homeleave ticket and per diem. You can either repay Peace Corps directly or have the money withdrawn from your readjustment allowance. Think hard before following this route, though. ET'ing in your third year vexes both the Peace Corps administration and other volunteers, because the extension process is competitive—meaning you beat someone out of a third-year spot who really wanted it, then quit.

62 Will I be overseas for the whole two years or can I come home in between?

Unless you foot the bill yourself, you are there for the whole two years. There is no R & R or homeleave for PCVs, with the exception of third-year extensions (see Question 61). You will have forty-eight vacation days during your volunteer service to use as you please. Several volunteers, including myself, came back to the States halfway through their two years for weddings, funerals, holidays, and the like. The costs of those trips, however, are the PCV's responsibility, and vacation days must be claimed.

Aside from extending, the only way to fly back to the States on the Peace Corps' tab is to get "medivacked" (medically evacuated). If you contract some deadly or bizarre disease, if you get pregnant, or if you injure yourself in such a manner that you can't be treated reasonably in-country, you may be medivacked to Washington, D.C. For more on medivacs, see Question 35.

63 Can I transfer programs if I don't like what I'm doing?

Not really. When you join the Peace Corps, you state in your application the skills and relevant areas in which you have experience. When you interview, you are evaluated and considered for a specific PC program area. When you go through training, you learn technical skills and practical methods to plan, implement, and evaluate projects in your program. If, during training, you decide you aren't interested in the program and can't envision yourself doing related project work for the next two years, the Peace Corps will most likely invite you to ET. If you get to post and start your projects, then months down the road come in to the office and voice similar complaints, the Peace Corps will still most likely invite you to ET. They may be able to offer you another post, but there usually isn't much they can offer in the way of other programs.

There are some extenuating circumstances that may allow you to change programs, however. For example, in my country of service there was a nationwide teachers' strike which resulted in the closing of all public schools for almost a year. This left the Peace Corps in a bind since a quarter of all volunteers in-country were education volunteers. At first, affected PCVs were advised to wait out the strike and start secondary projects in the meantime. When it became apparent that the strike was going to last more than a month or two, and volunteers were starting to ET en masse, volunteers were given some leeway in deciding if they wanted to switch programs, go to other countries, or return to the States. Those who chose to switch programs faced quite an ordeal, though. In most cases they had to change villages, undergo at least a month or two of programmatic training, and start their two years all over again.

My advice is to think hard about your assigned program area before going overseas with the Peace Corps. If you have any doubts about your commitment to the program, think about reapplying under a different one. If you are intent on going despite doubts about your interest level in the work, do your best to go into it with an open mind and a positive attitude. Also, talk to RPCVs who worked in your assigned field to find out what, exactly, your work will entail.

64 Can I transfer countries if I don't like where I am?

As with transferring programs, transferring countries is only done under extenuating circumstances. If, for example, your country of service is evacuated due to war or civil unrest, you may be given the opportunity to transfer to another Peace Corps country depending on the availability of positions. In my two years as a volunteer, I only witnessed one incident that resulted in the transfer of volunteers from one country to another. A country that bordered ours erupted in civil war and all of its volunteers were evacuated to my country of service. They were housed in the capital while the Peace Corps figured out a "next step." As it happened, the evacuated volunteers were given a few options. Those who were close to COS'ing were offered early COS dates, and many of them left Cameroon to go directly back to the States. Those who were relatively new volunteers were given the opportunity to transfer to another country, as dictated by the availability of positions, and start their two years over again. Or they could return to the States through the Peace Corps' "discontinuance of service" process (a kind of honorable discharge from the organization).

The only other real opportunity PCVs have to transfer countries comes when they extend for a third year. With a great deal of effort, volunteers can seek out openings in other Peace Corps countries and apply for positions within their program area. To negotiate the transfer successfully, interested PCVs must contact appropriate CDs and maintain a similar level of persistence as was required during the initial PC application process. If you find yourself interested in attempting a third-year transfer, start the process early in your second year to ensure enough time for all the information exchange and application reviews. It's neither an easy nor common feat, but it's not altogether impossible.

65 Will I have access to embassy, commissary, and American Club services?

While you are overseas, you will quickly learn all about the "haves" and "have nots" by comparing your life with that of the embassy diplomats around you. You will be living in rudimentary structures with minimal amenities; they will be living in marble mansions with guards, servants, drivers, and gardeners. You will be eating local food and shopping in local markets; they will be eating American food and shopping in the commissary. You will go to your neighbor's house for entertainment, to listen to stories and learn customary dances and songs; they will go to the American Club for entertainment, to play tennis, grab a burger, and watch the latest movies on a big-screen TV.

At first, the decadent or detached life of the diplomats may confuse you. You'll marvel at the limited extent to which many embassy personnel interact with host country nationals, especially in comparison with your experiences. You'll ponder the efficacy and purpose of an institution seemingly isolated or out of touch with the realities of the country it purports to aid and assist. Then, you'll come in from the bush one day, go to the American Club (assuming USAID has a presence and has constructed one in your country), and all that confusion will morph into envy and appreciation.

If there is an American Club at the U.S. embassy, Peace Corps volunteers are usually granted access, which, you'll come to realize, is a real gift and gracious gesture. Typically, only embassy diplomats and Peace Corps staff have automatic Club privileges. Everyone else must be accompanied by a paying member to use the facilities. American Clubs have snack bars (serving burgers, ice cream, and American candy), swimming pools, TV rooms with a video library and a satellite hooked up to AFRTS (an army station that broadcasts everything from *Good Morning America* to *Star Trek: The Next Generation*), and tennis courts. If you are posted to a small, rural village, far removed from all that is American and familiar, you will appreciate the luxury of the Club when you come in to the capital to take care of Peace Corps business.

As for the rest of the embassy (the embassy restaurant, the money-changing desk, the commissary, the computer labs, the medical and mail services, etc.), Peace Corps volunteers are usually denied access. In smaller programs or countries, there may be a closer relationship between the embassy and the Peace Corps, in which case you may interact and have more embassy privileges. For the most part, however, don't count on being treated as a diplomat or allowed the same access to the embassy that diplomats have.

Part XI
Traveling Like a Pro

66 Will I have the opportunity to travel much during my two years as a volunteer?

Officially, PCVs are allowed two vacation days per month—forty-eight days for two years—to use as they please. The Peace Corps imposes only a few restrictions on those vacation days, which are 1) vacation request forms must be submitted to program directors for approval; 2) vacation days must be earned before they are claimed; and 3) volunteers must refrain from vacationing during their first three months at post (to facilitate acculturation, integration, and the establishment of work and projects).

As a volunteer serving for two years in a foreign and often exotic country, however, you are guaranteed to encounter travel opportunities that conflict with the Peace Corps' policies. In those situations, think carefully before throwing caution to the wind. On the one hand, most volunteers take at least a few unofficial vacations, called "clando" (as in "clandestine") trips, during their time in the Peace Corps. On the other hand, if you are caught, be prepared for anything from a reprimand to an administrative separation.

Clando trips aside, you should find that opportunities to travel during your Peace Corps service are profuse. In my opinion, there is little excuse to spend two years in one country without seeing all there is to see. Take the time, plan the trips, get some folks together, and do it.

If you're thinking about traveling outside your country of service during your two years, you'll need to plan, budget, and prepare more carefully than for domestic trips, but it can easily be done. Of course, you shouldn't make your international trip one of your clando adventures—it's a sure-fire way to get thrown out of the Peace Corps, and it's dangerous to boot. During my second year of service, I took three weeks of official vacation to travel through three West African countries with a group of friends. Others I knew flew to Kenya for a month, checked out South Africa, met their folks in London for Christmas, flew back to the States for a wedding, and so on. If you have the time and means, such trips are worthwhile breaks from Peace Corps life, and offer adventures and opportunities you may not encounter without leaving your country of service.

In any Peace Corps program, there are always a handful of volunteers who refrain from taking trips of any kind, preferring to stay in their villages instead. In truth, they are often better integrated, slightly more productive, and feel more at home in their local communities that most. On the other hand, they fail to attain a more holistic impression of their country of service, and miss out on various cultural and social opportunities their fellow volunteers enjoy. Different strokes for different folks—it just goes to show there is no right or wrong approach to the Peace Corps experience.

67 Can I travel to other countries after my Peace Corps service is over?

Yes, you can. In fact, post–Peace Corps travel is oft cited as one of the main reasons people join the Peace Corps to begin with. When you complete your service (COS), you will be offered the choice of receiving a Peace Corps–issued one-way ticket back to your permanent home of record in the States, or receiving the cash value of that ticket in either U.S. dollars or the local currency. Since Uncle Sam buys full-fare, refundable, flexible tickets, those one-way fares are usually worth a lot of money. Many RPCVs take the "cash in lieu of" (as it's often referred to in the Peace Corps) and purchase tickets to various exotic destinations around the world.

You will also receive one-third of your readjustment allowance ($2,025) in the form of a U.S. government treasury check upon COS'ing—an amount sufficient to finance your travels after purchasing the plane tickets with your "cash in lieu of" money. Traveling post-PC can be especially low-budget considering you will have just spent two years perfecting the art of shoestring living in your village. Also, as a newly COS'ed volunteer, you can plug into the PCV network wherever you travel, staying in rest houses and PCVs' homes, gaining unique insights into other countries and forging new friendships along the way.

Many wonder why some COS'ing volunteers take the PC-issued return ticket home and forgo the chance to jet around the world as only an RPCV can. There are several reasons. Many volunteers, as they approach their COS date, begin to appreciate the magnitude of the challenges that lie ahead of them in terms of readjustment to life in the States. Knowing that they face indefinite unemployment and a renewed dependence on mom and dad, if even for a month or two, can be incredibly depressing. In that state of mind, jetting around the world may seem like delaying the inevitable, and perhaps worsening it by burning through your readjustment allowance before you really need it.

Others are comfortable with the thought of moving back home, but are anxious to start their job search or prepare for graduate school. Some are simply fed up with living like bohemians and find no appeal in the thought of backpacking around, living like a grub for another six months. They figure they've spent two years living an adventurous, tumultuous, unpredictable life, and welcome the opportunity to construct a sensible, stable, structured life back in the States.

68 Will I be issued a diplomatic passport?

No, you will not be issued a diplomatic (a.k.a. "black") passport. You will, however, have a special note on the inside of your passport indicating that you are a Peace Corps volunteer, which helps distinguish you from a tourist and often results in a certain degree of preferential treatment (particularly when dealing with customs officials, border crossings, and local police).

The difference between a regular U.S. passport, which Peace Corps volunteers are issued, and a diplomatic one is substantial. Carriers of diplomatic passports are essentially "above the law." They cannot be prosecuted by local officials for breaching local (national) laws. They are granted immunities and embassy privileges which other Americans overseas are denied.

Aside from your passport, however, you will be issued an official Peace Corps identification card once you swear in as a volunteer. Your Peace Corps ID may not wield as much power as a passport, but it will certainly wield as much influence in many parts of the world. While it's not practical to carry your passport with you at all times during your Peace Corps service (in fact, it's best to store it in the Peace Corps safe), you should carry your Peace Corps ID religiously. Most officials in countries where the Peace Corps works are familiar with the organization and its structure. As such, your ID card will suffice during routine stops, checks, or crossings.

Part XII
Post-Peace Corps

69 How hard is readjusting to life back in the States?

If you are thinking of joining the Peace Corps, or you have already been accepted and are waiting to leave, readjustment to life in the States after your service is probably the last thing on your mind. In fact, if someone asked you about it, you'd probably laugh and say, "What is there to readjust to?" Well, for those of you who are foresighted enough to wonder and to worry about this issue, I'll address it briefly now.

In short, readjustment is as difficult as, if not more difficult than, adjusting to life overseas. Once you have spent two years in the Peace Corps, you have adapted both externally and internally. You have changed the way you think, perceive, react, converse, analyze, expect, dream, live, digest, and learn. You have modified your behavior to adapt to an extreme circumstance—so much so that the extreme becomes mundane, and you no longer feel alienated from a culture so distant from the one you left behind in the States.

When your two years are up and you come back home, the vastness and breadth of your experience and the ways in which it affected you become glaringly obvious. What you once thought would be easy and effortless is suddenly as impossible and intimidating as moving overseas once was—only worse because you didn't expect it. Even though "reverse culture shock" is touched on during your COS conference, and stories of readjustment hell are abundant in the overseas volunteer community, you won't appreciate the challenges that lie ahead of you until you reach the States.

It's not just about reacclimating to the weather, the food, the fast pace of life, and the rigid social environment. It's about realizing that your life is suddenly in your own hands again. Two years in the Peace Corps' cradling arm, though seemingly invisible at times during your service, will have spoiled you. And when that arm jettisons you out toward the glass and concrete of mainstream U.S.A., you'll inevitably feel disoriented.

Most RPCVs, having joined the Peace Corps soon after graduating from college, return to the States without a job or a place to live. As such, the rigors of emotional readjustment are compounded by the need for physical and financial readjustment. Others, however, manage to line up grad school or employment offers before they COS. For these lucky few, all of the mental and emotional hurdles discussed above apply, but are mitigated somewhat by the structure that awaits them. Regardless of an RPCV's level of preparedness, the nature of transitioning back to life in the States requires certain adjustments that simply can't be avoided: acknowledging that your own culture feels somewhat alien to you; shifting perspective to accommodate the wealth of American society; changing mental gears to join the breakneck pace of the developed world; and so on.

For the typical RPCV (i.e., one who returns to the States unsure of the "next step") readjustment seems to follow a pattern. It starts with elation as you embrace your family and plop on the sofa to bask in being "home." After spending a few weeks telling stories and visiting old friends, stage two sets in: confusion with a dash of depression. You realize you've visited everyone, told your best stories, spent your readjustment allowance, and have begun to wear out the welcome mat at your parents' house. You also realize that, after catching up with friends, they went to work the next day, while you plopped on the couch again and watched TV.

Enter stage three: panic. You suddenly look around and realize that to truly reestablish yourself as a contributing member of society, you have to get a job. You need money, a place to live, a means of transport, and most importantly, a purpose in life. Unfortunately, not one of those is easy to come by. In fact, they require kicking, screaming, scrambling, and competing with other folks—a far cry from the requirements of everyday life back in your Peace Corps village. You feel at once anxious and overwhelmed, and you wonder how you could have ever thought coming home would be easy.

The remaining stages are similar to any you'd experience if you were recently graduating from college or switching jobs. They involve all the frustration, despair, elation, and anxiety that are normally associated with job searching. Each small step you take at this point brings you closer and closer to complete readjustment. In the end, when you are moved into your own apartment, you are gainfully employed, your credit cards are under control, and you no longer freak out in grocery stores or mega-malls, you'll feel a deep satisfaction at what you've accomplished. You will have come full circle, but that circle will encompass an experience more personal and enriching than most can comprehend.

70

Does the Peace Corps look good on a resume? Will it help me get into graduate school?

As difficult as returning to the States may be, one thing you can count on to lessen the blow and boost your spirits is praise and admiration from everyone who knows or discovers that you are an RPCV. No matter how you feel about the Peace Corps based on your personal experiences overseas, you'll most likely discover that the majority of Americans view the organization in a straightforward, overwhelmingly positive light. The more you speak to them of the Peace Corps' complexities and realities, the more you confirm their impression of the Peace Corps as something few Americans can endure.

Needless to say, the Peace Corps looks great on a resume and provides a nice stepping stone for any number of career paths you may decide to follow. Oftentimes your program and project accomplishments won't even matter—potential employers will see that you served in the Peace Corps and conclude that you are dependable, determined, confident, adaptable, resourceful, and personable. If your overseas experience actually fits the requirements of the position for which you are applying, the stepping stone is that much higher. I've never heard an RPCV speak of the Peace Corps as a detriment to his or her resume.

Another way that the Peace Corps can help land you a job is through an extensive RPCV network. Once you start job-searching, you'll quickly realize that RPCVs are everywhere—the public sector, the private sector, NGOs, and so on. With the help of the Peace Corps' Returned Volunteer Services Office, you can tap into the RPCV community to expand and expedite your job search.

Your Peace Corps experience puts you head and shoulders over other applicants for graduate school as well, for all the reasons I cited above. You will stand out as an individual who has learned about the world in a way few others have—a valuable contribution to any course of study. You will have demonstrated that you have personality traits necessary to tackle graduate programs with commitment and determination. You will have proven that you possess an acute ability to absorb, process, learn, solve problems creatively, and thrive under adverse and challenging conditions—something few graduate admissions offices fail to appreciate.

In addition, Peace Corps has established cooperative relationships with select graduate schools to offer Master's International programs to those interested in pursuing advanced degrees in conjunction with their Peace Corps service. As a Master's International student, you can receive up to twelve credits for your two years overseas, and apply those credits toward any number of graduate programs in fields as varied as business, public health and nutrition, and forestry. Typically, students complete one year of intensive graduate study at a participating institution, then head overseas to begin their Peace Corps assignments. For more information on the Master's International program, refer to Appendix G.

71

What is "noncompetitive eligibility" and what can it do for me?

Noncompetitive eligibility (NCE) gives you special hiring consideration for federal government jobs. It identifies you as an "insider," on par with current federal employees in the eyes of human resource departments and the Office of Personnel Management (OPM). As such, NCE qualifies you for positions that may be closed to the general public (known as "merit promotion" positions), virtually doubling the number of job opportunities available to you. It also exempts you from having to be the best qualified candidate for a given job; rather, you are only required to meet the minimum qualifications as specified in a vacancy announcement. In essence, NCE allows you to be more proactive in your federal job search by opening more doors and eliminating a few layers of bureaucracy. All RPCVs are granted NCE for one year from their COS date. Under certain circumstances, and with prior approval, extensions may be granted.

If you work for the federal government after the Peace Corps, your volunteer service will help in other ways, too. If your new duties and responsibilities directly relate to your Peace Corps experience, you may qualify for a higher grade or step, translating to increased pay. You will have two years' credit toward retirement and vacation hours earned per pay period. You will also have access to an astonishing network of RPCVs in the federal system who can help advance your career in more subtle ways.

If you have questions about NCE and the ways it can be used to your advantage should you decide to pursue government work, don't hesitate to contact the Returned Volunteer Services Office at the Peace Corps and speak with a career counselor. It's a unique and valuable perk; don't let it go to waste!

72 Can I bring my Peace Corps pet back to the States with me?

Yes, but it could take more time and money to send ol' Spot back to Cleveland than you may think. Understanding that some people get really attached to their pets, I'll try not to discourage the practice of bringing them back to the States. But think hard about it before jumping in with both feet. Remember that there are plenty of homeless pets in the U.S. that are just begging to be adopted, and that any pet born and bred overseas may suffer before acclimating to a more restrictive life in the States. Peace Corps pets generally have free reign at volunteers' posts—they know no leash laws, city sidewalks, busy streets, small yards, animal pounds, or dog houses—quite a difference from pet life in this country, unless you happen to live on a ranch in Wyoming.

If you are intent on bringing a pet back with you, you'll need to contact the Ministry of Agriculture to purchase a "pet export license." Cost will vary from country to country, as will processing time. You'll also need to take your pet to a U.S.-certified veterinarian (the embassy can you provide you a list), and have the animal checked out and vaccinated. If the veterinarian is not U.S. certified, your pet's health records will not be admitted by custom officials in the States. Lastly, contact the airline and inquire about costs and regulations associated with pet transport. Volunteers I spoke with who went through this process mentioned that airports in several countries prohibit the loading of animals onto planes when the tarmac is over eighty degrees Fahrenheit. On dry season days, which constitute half the year in much of the developing world, the tarmac can get even hotter than that, so keep those kinds of rules in mind when booking your flight.

73

Would you go back and do the Peace Corps all over again?

"Yes, I would join again and actually plan to join again with my husband once I retire. I feel like I have much more to offer now. The first time around I learned a lot. Next time around I hope to be able to teach a lot."
Ann Swanberg-Mee, Kenya (1989–1991)

"Based on my experience I would definitely do the Peace Corps if I had never done it. I would not have missed it for the world. On the other hand, having done it, I have no desire to repeat it. While I expect to return to the country where I served, I prefer to travel in a little more comfort these days."
Richard Louthan, Cameroon (1993–1997)

"Yes, I would do it all over again. The personal growth I experienced while adapting to a foreign working and living environment was invaluable. I built water systems and helped people who were not being helped by their government, which felt good in and of itself, but I also benefited personally and professionally from my Peace Corps experience."
Karl Banks, Ecuador (1994–1996)

"Having already completed one 'tour of duty,' I probably would not join the PC again unless it was with a partner (i.e., husband) down the road. I can definitely say that I'm glad I had my PC experience and would undoubtedly do it over again if I could go back in time. It was clearly the most difficult thing I have ever done, but a very positive experience overall."
Laura Gentile, Philippines (1988–1990)

"One hundred and ten percent yes. Why? Because I grew more in those two years than in any other period of my life. I emerged from the Peace Corps older, wiser, and with a breadth of cultural understanding and awareness that serves me well every single day. In fact, I would go back for the language training alone. 'Learn Arabic in ten weeks'—sounds like a bad late-night infomercial . . . but with the Peace Corps it's true."
Rob Peterson, Tunisia (1994–1996)

"If I could, I'd go back and do the 'experience' all over again but the 'Peace Corps' part of it was the most frustrating and least rewarding. I will always be grateful to the Peace Corps for giving me the opportunity to do the work I did in Uzbekistan and for placing me in my host community, but they were often a hindrance to my work. I saw the Peace Corps' bureaucracy undermine many volunteers, professionally and personally, and some of my experiences with the PC medical office were horrific. Just as I feel passionate about Uzbekistan, I also feel passionate about the Peace Corps; there's so much to love and hate about them both. I think that people who are drawn to living and working overseas are attracted to living life in such extremes—extremes you just can't find in the States. One thing's for sure: if you can handle the Peace Corps, you can handle the third world!"
Anne Hauk, Uzbekistan (1994–1996)

"The short answer to that question is yes! Working and living with the people of Paraguay was a life-enriching experience in many ways. I would certainly go back and do it all over again and I encourage those who have an interest in service, in other cultures, and in self-discovery to join the Peace Corps. I would, however, counsel married couples to examine their motives and motivations before joining. My wife's experience was not as positive as mine—she had really hoped to learn Spanish, which was all but impossible in our rural village. Women are treated much differently in Paraguay than in the U.S., as well. Even so, she really connected with the community through her outgoing personality. In the final analysis, people who are positive, open-minded, resilient, and willing to work with their communities will be amply rewarded by serving in the Peace Corps."
Nick Spraig, Paraguay (1994–1995)

"My thinking on this has changed from when I first returned. Back then, I was very glad to have volunteered, but didn't think I'd ever sign up again. I felt like it took too long in the Peace Corps to 'get up to speed' and start feeling productive. Now, however, I feel like I could contribute more and be more effective, though I'm less amenable to forsaking the creature comforts of home and struggling to learn a new language. I do occasionally think about volunteering again, and would definitely do it the same way if I had to go back and do it all over."
Jack Landy, Thailand (1981–1984)

"Yes, I would do it all over again and probably will! The cross-cultural exchange between me and my family, students, teachers, and friends was one of the best experiences of my life. I truly feel I made an impact on my students' English abilities and their understanding of American culture. I grew as an individual and would welcome the opportunity to challenge myself again by volunteering in the future."
Ellen P. Kelly, Armenia (1992–1994)

"Yes! The entire experience taught me to look at the world differently and appreciate aspects of my own country and culture that I had never before valued. I cannot put a value on the many relationships I established with people in my community and other Peace Corps volunteers. It was also an opportunity to be completely autonomous in every aspect of my life."
Scott Stollman, Costa Rica (1995–1997)

"The Peace Corps offers a unique experience in that volunteers are able to immerse themselves in the village environment, learn local languages and traditions, integrate appropriate, locally available resources, forge some niche for themselves over a two- to three-year service, yet remain confident that, in the case of evacuation or medical emergency, the Peace Corps will assist them. I would not hesitate to return to the Peace Corps and the simplicity of my life during those four years—the inner tranquillity one attains with a sense of true priorities, sincere friendships, and communal support."
Leigh Lentile, Niger (1992–1994), Cameroon (1994–1996)

"I would definitely do the Peace Corps again, especially now that I am older and have more experience under my belt. I was so young when I volunteered; I think I got much more out of it than I gave. I would love to experience the satisfaction of 'hands-on' work again, develop the lifetime relationships with women so different from myself, and breathe wonderfully fresh air every day as I did in Morocco. I have not felt so satisfied with a job since the Peace Corps. I really know I made a difference there—it has been much harder to feel that way since I returned. Every day in the Peace Corps brought a new adventure, whether it was a lively conversation with the woman next door, a wild boar running through town, or helping the local vet give animals vaccinations. The whole experience for me was full of wonder—and I know my neighbors sure wondered about me!"
Amy Gambrill, Morocco (1993–1995)

Appendices

Peace Corps General Facts

The Mission of the Peace Corps
To help the people of interested countries in meeting their need for trained men and women. To help promote a better understanding of Americans on the part of the peoples served. To help promote a better understanding of other peoples on the part of Americans.

History
Peace Corps Officially Established: March 1, 1961
Total Number of Volunteers and Trainees to Date: 152,000
Total Number of Countries Served: 134

Volunteers
Current Number of Volunteers and Trainees: 6,700

Gender:	60% female, 40% male
Marital Status:	90% single, 10% married
Minorities:	14% of Peace Corps volunteers
Average Age:	29 years old
Volunteers over 50:	7% of Peace Corps volunteers
Oldest Volunteer:	78 years old
Education:	15% graduate studies/degrees 80% undergraduate degrees

Countries
Current Number of Countries Served: 80
New Countries Served in 1998: Bangladesh, Mozambique

Projects
Volunteers by Sector: Education (39%), Environment (17%), Health (17%), Business (13%), Agriculture (9%), Other (5%)

FY '99 Budget: $241 million

Recruitment Toll-Free Number: 1-800-424-8580

Website: http://www.peacecorps.gov

Revised 2/99

Peace Corps Country Map

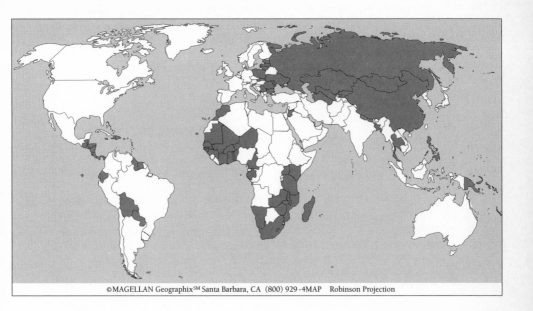

©MAGELLAN Geographix℠ Santa Barbara, CA (800) 929-4MAP   Robinson Projection

AFRICA
Benin, Burkina Faso, Cameroon, Cape Verde, Gabon, The Gambia, Ghana, Guinea, Ivory Coast, Kenya, Lesotho, Madagascar, Malawi, Mali, Mauritania, Mozambique, Namibia, Niger, Senegal, South Africa, Tanzania, Togo, Zambia, Zimbabwe

INTER-AMERICA AND THE CARIBBEAN
Antigua/Barbuda, Belize, Bolivia, Costa Rica, Dominica, Dominican Republic, Grenada & Carriacou, Ecuador, El Salvador, Grenadines & St. Vincent, Guatemala, Guyana, Haiti, Honduras, Jamaica, Nicaragua, Panama, Paraguay, St. Kitts/Nevis, St. Lucia, Suriname

CENTRAL AND EAST ASIA
Bangladesh, China, Kazakhstan, Kyrgyz Republic, Mongolia, Nepal, Thailand, Turkmenistan, Uzbekistan

EUROPE AND THE MEDITERRANEAN
Armenia, Bulgaria, Estonia, Jordan, Latvia, Lithuania, Moldova, Morocco, Poland, Romania, Russia, Slovakia, Ukraine

THE PACIFIC
Kiribati, Micronesia, Niue, Palau, Papua New Guinea, Philippines, Samoa, Solomon Islands, Tonga, Vanuatu

Peace Corps Programs and Requirements

The following is a complete list of Peace Corps Programs and the general requirements needed to qualify. Remember, Peace Corps service is possible, even if you don't "fit" exactly into these categories. Liberal arts majors and "generalists" are encouraged to apply. Contact your Peace Corps recruiter at (800) 424-8580 to discuss how your educational and/or work experiences apply to these programs.

ENVIRONMENT

100 Forestry
A. BA/BS any degree plus three years responsible work experience in forestry or nursery management, or
B. BS/AS Forestry or Watershed Management, or
C. BS/AS Natural Resources, Environmental Science, or Ecology, or
D. BS Biology, Botany, Ornamental Horticulture, or Geology with six months growing experience or field work (nursery, greenhouse, gardening, farming).

103 Parks and Wildlife
A. BS Wildlife Biology or Wildlife Management, or
B. BA/BS Resource Management or Recreation/Park Administration, or
C. BA/BS any degree plus three years work experience in Park Planning/Administration, Resource Management, or Wildlife Management.

104 Environmental Education/Awareness
A. BA/BS Environmental Education, or
B. BA/BS Environmental Science, Environmental Studies, Environmental Interpretation, Natural Resources, Conservation, or Ecology, with expressed interest in promoting environmental awareness in school and communities or

C. BA/BS any discipline with two years professional experience organizing/leading environmental education activities, or
D. BA/BS any environmental discipline with a minimum of six months experience organizing/leading environmental activities, and expressed interest in promoting environmental awareness in schools and communities.

107 Community Forestry Extension
A. Demonstrated ability in planning, organizing, counseling, or leadership within the past four years, and a minimum of five seasons practical growing experience (nursery, greenhouse, farming, gardening), or
B. BA/BS any discipline with a minimum of 8 semester hours/12 quarter hours in botany, natural resources, ornamental horticulture, environmental education, parks and recreation, agronomy, forestry, or geology, PLUS three months experience in farming, gardening, nursery work, tree planting, tree care, or urban forestry, or
C. BA/BS any discipline with demonstrated ability in planning, organizing, counseling, or leadership in the past four years AND with six months experience in farming, gardening, nursery work/management, tree planting, tree care, or urban forestry.

AGRICULTURE

101 Fisheries
A. BS Fisheries (freshwater or marine) or any biological science, or
B. BA/BS any discipline with a minimum of 8 semester/12 quarter hours in biology and/or chemistry.

110 Crop Extension
A. BS/AS Agronomy, Horticulture or other agricultural discipline, or
B. Three years full-time farm experience, or
C. BA/BS any discipline with eighteen months full-time farm experience

113 Agriculture Education
A. BS Agriculture Education, or
B. BA/BS any education discipline with two years farm experience, or
C. BA/BS any agriculture discipline with an expressed interest in teaching, or
D. BA/BS any discipline with two years farm experience and an expressed interest in teaching, or
E. BA/BS any discipline with a minimum of 15 semester/22 quarter hours in agriculture-related courses and an expressed interest in teaching agriculture, or
F. BS Biology or General Science with an expressed interest in teaching agriculture.

114 Farm Management/ Agribusiness
A. BA/BS Agriculture Economics, or
B. Three years experience in farm management and/or agribusiness, or
C. BA/BS degree combining agricultural AND management, including agribusiness, agricultural management, farm management, or
D. BA/BS any business or economics discipline with one year experience in farming or agribusiness.

115 Animal Husbandry
A. BS/AS Animal Husbandry, Animal Science or Poultry Science, or
B. Three consecutive years farm experience working with livestock, or
C. BS/BA any discipline with eighteen months farm experience working with livestock.

117 Community Agriculture Extension
Demonstrated ability in planning, organizing, counseling, or leadership within the past four years AND
A. BA/BS any discipline with a minimum of three months experience in vegetable gardening, or
B. Six months experience in farm-related activities, vegetable gardening, 4-H, FFA, or FHA.

COMMUNITY DEVELOPMENT

122 General Construction
A. Two years work experience in general construction, masonry, carpentry, or plumbing, or
B. BA/BS any discipline with six months (two summers) work experience in general construction, masonry, carpentry, or plumbing.

160 Home Economics
A. BA/BS Home Economics or Human Ecology with the ability to teach traditional Home Economics coursework, or
B. BA/BS any discipline with demonstrated interest in cooking, sewing, or other Home Economics-related areas, and an expressed interest in teaching Home Economics, or
C. No degree but has raised a family. Must have sewing, cooking and other homemaking skills and an expressed interest in teaching such skills.

162 Community Services

Demonstrated ability in planning, organizing, counseling, or leadership within the past five years AND

A. BA/BS in Social Work, Social Services, Counseling or Community Development, or

B. BA/BS in any discipline.

164 Urban Youth Development

A. BA/BS any discipline and six months full-time work experience with at-risk youth (youth out of work or out of school) between the ages of 10 and 25 in a youth-oriented organization, or

B. AA/AS any discipline and one year full-time work experience in youth leadership training or in directing youth programs for at-risk youth (youth out of work or out of school) between the ages of 10 and 25 in a youth-oriented organization, or

C. Five years full-time experience with at-risk youth (youth out of work or out of school) between the ages of 10 and 25 in a youth-oriented organization.

HEALTH

124 Hygiene Education/Sanitation

Demonstrated ability in planning, organizing, counseling, or leadership within the past four years AND

A. One year work experience in construction, masonry, carpentry or plumbing, or

B. BA/BS any discipline with expressed interest in hygiene education/sanitation and a demonstrated interest in hands-on skilled work (mechanical repairs, construction, carpentry, set design, etc.).

131 Environmental And Water Resources Engineering

A. Certification in water/waste water treatment plant operation or hazardous materials management, or

B. BA/BS Civil Engineering with 12 semester hours of environmental engineering–related coursework, or

C. BA/BS Environmental or Sanitary Engineering, or

D. MA/MS Environmental or Sanitary Engineering, or Civil Engineering with an environmental emphasis.

150 Nursing

Currently Registered Nurse (RN) AND

A. BS in Nursing, or

B. Three-year nursing diploma, or

C. AA in Nursing.

154 Health Degrees

A. Masters in Public Health (not including concentration in Health Service Administration or Biostatistics), or

B. Certified Physician's Assistant with an expressed interest in public/community health, or

C. BA/BS Nutrition or Health.

155 Health Extension

Demonstrated ability in planning, organizing, counseling, or leadership within the past four years AND

A. BA/BS in any discipline with a demonstrated interest in health (e.g., Red Cross, EMT, or CPR certification; hospital or clinic experience; Planned Parenthood counseling or lab tech experience), or

B. LPN/LVN with two years post-license experience.

BUSINESS

134 Urban and Regional Planning
A. BA/BS or MA/MS Urban/Regional Planning, or
B. MA/MS Public Administration or Public Policy with Urban Planning emphasis, or
C. BA/BS Architecture, Urban Studies or Geography AND one year Urban Planning experience, or
D. BA/BS any discipline with five years professional experience (three years directly related to urban planning).

140 Business Advising
A. Four years experience as the manager of a business, or
B. AA any business discipline (not including economics) with two years experience as the manager of a business, or
C. BA/BS any business discipline (not including economics), or
D. BA/BS Economics.

141 Cooperatives
A. Four years work experience in coops, credit unions, small business, or bookkeeping, or
B. AA/AS any discipline with two years work experience in coops, credit unions, small business, or bookkeeping, or
C. BA/BS any discipline with one year work experience in coops, credit unions, small business, or bookkeeping, or
D. BA/BS any business or economics discipline.

142 Accounting
A. Three years work experience in accounting, or
B. Certified Public Accountant, or
C. BA any business or economics discipline with one year work experience in accounting, or
D. AA Accounting with two years work experience in accounting, or

E. BA/BS Accounting.

143 Computer Science
A. BA/BS Computer Science or Information Systems, or
B. Minimum five years experience in programming, systems analysis, systems design, consulting in computer field, or
C. BA/BS any discipline with minor (15 semester/22 quarter hours) in computer science and two years related experience, or
D. AA computer-related discipline with two years computer experience.

144 Business Development
A. MBA, MA/MS in Business Administration, Public Administration, Management, Accounting, Banking, or Finance, or
B. BA/BS Business Administration, Management, Accounting, Banking, Finance, or Public Administration PLUS a minimum of two years full-time business-related experience, or
C. BA/BS any discipline PLUS five years full-time business-related experience, or
D. Component A with two years business experience PLUS one year business teaching experience, or Component B PLUS one year business teaching experience, or Component C PLUS one year business teaching experience.

145 NGO Development
A. BA/BS any discipline and two years full-time management or organizational development experience with nonprofit organizations, or
B. BA/BS any discipline and two years experience in a leadership role (involved in long-term organizational and resource development) or a nonprofit organization, or

C. Master's degree with an emphasis in nonprofit management, public administration, or organizational development, or
D. Five years full-time management or organizational development experience with nonprofit organizations.

EDUCATION

120 Vocational Education
A. BA/BS Industrial Arts or Technical Education, or
B. AA/AS Industrial Arts or Technical Education with one year related work experience, or
C. Technical diploma from a post-secondary school in cabinet making, machining, plumbing, carpentry, electricity, welding, or metalworking with two years work experience, or
D. Eighteen months work experience in cabinet making, machining, plumbing, carpentry, electricity, welding, or metalworking, or
E. BA/BS any discipline with six months work experience in cabinet making, machining, plumbing, carpentry, electricity, welding, or metalworking.

170 Primary Education Teacher Training
A. BA/BS Pre-school, Early Childhood, Elementary Education PLUS one or more years of teaching experience, or
B. BA/BS Pre-school, Early Childhood or Elementary Education, or
C. BA/BS any discipline with elementary education certification, or
D. BA/BS any discipline with one or more years of teaching experience at the Early Childhood or Elementary level.

171 Secondary Education TEFL/English Training
A. BA/BS Secondary Education with concentration in English, TEFL, or foreign language, or
B. BA/BS any discipline with secondary education certification to teach English, TEFL, or a foreign language, or
C. BA/BS English, TEFL, or Linguistics, or
D. BA/BS any discipline with at least three months of English or foreign language tutoring, or adult literacy experience.

172 University English Teaching
A. MA English, TEFL, or Linguistics, or
B. MA French, or
C. MA any other foreign language.

173 Secondary Education Math Teaching
A. BA/BS Secondary Education with concentration in math, or
B. BA/BS any discipline with secondary education certification in math, or
C. BA/BS Math, or
D. BA/BS Engineering or Computer Science, or
E. BA/BS any discipline with a minor (15 semester hours/22 quarter hours) in math. Applicants must have at least two college calculus courses (not including pre-calculus).

175 Secondary Education Science Teaching
A. BA/BS Secondary Education with concentration in any science, or
B. BA/BS any discipline with secondary education certification in science, or
C. BA/BS General Science, Biology, Chemistry, or Physics, or
D. BA/BS Engineering, any physical science or any biological science, or

E. BA/BS any discipline with a minor (15 semester hours/22 quarter hours) in Biology, Chemistry, or Physics.

177 Special Education

A. BA/BS Special Education (general or with vision- or hearing-impaired emphasis), or
B. BA/BS any discipline with secondary education certification in special education (general or with emphasis in vision- or hearing-impaired), or
C. BA/BS Education with one year full-time experience working with persons who are learning disabled, developmentally disabled, emotionally handicapped, physically handicapped, multiply handicapped, hearing-impaired, or visually-impaired, or
D. BA/BS any discipline with one year full-time experience working with persons who are learning disabled, developmentally disabled, emotionally handicapped, physically handicapped, multiply handicapped, hearing-impaired, or vision-impaired.

183 Visual and Performing Arts

A. BA/BS Education (primary or secondary) with a concentration in Art, Fine Arts, Visual Arts, Music, Dramatic/Theater Arts, Performing Arts, or
B. BA/BS any discipline plus primary or secondary certification in Art, Fine Arts, Music, Dramatic/Theater Arts, or Performing Arts, or
C. BA/BS Art, Fine Arts, Visual Arts, Music, Dramatic/Theater Arts, Performing Arts plus an expressed interest in formal or nonformal education outreach.

184 Library Science

A. MA/MS Library Science, or
B. BA/BS Library Science with one year related work experience.

190 Physical Education/Youth Work

A. BA/BS Physical Education or Recreation, or
B. BA/BS any discipline with at least three months of coaching experience.

191 Secondary Education English Teacher Training

A. MAT English, TEFL or foreign language, Applied Linguistics, or
B. MEd with graduate or undergraduate concentration in English, TEFL, or foreign language, or
C. BA/BS Secondary Education with concentration in English, TEFL, or foreign language, or
D. BA/BS any discipline with secondary education certification in English, TEFL, or foreign language, or
E. BA/BS English, TEFL, or foreign language with six months teaching experience at the secondary level in English, or foreign language, or
F. BA/BS any discipline with one year teaching experience at the secondary level in English, TEFL, or foreign language.

193 Secondary Education Math Teacher Training

A. MAT Math, or
B. MA Education with graduate or undergraduate concentration in math, or
C. BA/BS Secondary Education with concentration in math, or
D. BA/BS any discipline with secondary education certification in math, or
E. BA/BS Math with six months teaching experience at the secondary level in math, or
F. BA/BS any discipline with one year of teaching experience at the secondary level in math.

195 Secondary Education Science Teacher Training

A. MAT specific science subject, or
B. MA Education with graduate or undergraduate concentration in specific science subject, or
C. BA/BS Secondary Education with concentration in specific science subject, or
D. BA/BS any discipline with secondary education certification in specific science subject, or
E. BA/BS specific science with six months teaching experience at the secondary level in that specific science, or
F. BA/BS any discipline with one year of teaching experience at the secondary level in a specific science subject.

FOR YOUR INFORMATION

1. In almost all cases, only language study or coursework gained within the past ten years will be considered when determining an applicant's qualifications for assignments.

2. *Demonstrated interest* in a program means that an applicant has acquired at least three months of experience through employment, hobbies, volunteer work, organizations joined, etc., OR has taken at least 8 semester (12 quarter) credit hours in appropriate courses. *Expressed interest* is a statement by the applicant indicating an interest in working for two years in a particular program.

3. Many of the requests we receive require the applicant to have studied Spanish or French (a) for two years in high school; (b) for two semesters in college; or (c) for six months while living in a community where that language is spoken.

4. With few exceptions, Education assignments require a minimum 2.5 GPA in the qualifying subjects.

5. A minor is defined as 15 semester hours or 22 quarter hours.

6. Married couples without dependents may apply. However, few positions are available, so placement of couples is always difficult.

7. Your competitiveness as an applicant can be enhanced by
   a. Foreign language study, especially in Spanish or French
   b. Teaching or tutoring experience in English, Math, or Science
   c. Paid or volunteer work experience, as applicable to programs
   d. Ability to lead, organize, and motivate people.

8. We suggest you return your application at least a year prior to your availability date.

Revised 4/16/97

How to Become a Competitive Candidate

"How hard is it to get in?" is one of the most common questions Peace Corps recruiters hear. The Peace Corps application process is competitive, just like it would be for any employer, but it is a myth that liberal arts majors are not wanted or do not quality for Peace Corps service!

The truth is that the Peace Corps welcomes and encourages people with degrees in the humanities and social sciences to apply. Volunteers with these backgrounds generally are placed in community-based programs in English teaching, health, agriculture and forestry, youth development, and community services.

With a bachelor's degree in any discipline and the experience and/or coursework listed below, you may qualify for the following Peace Corps programs.

IF YOU ARE INTERESTED IN:	YOU WILL NEED:
English Teaching	Three to six months of English or foreign language tutoring in a structured program that provides training. Your student(s) must be at least 12 years old, and you must complete at least ten hours of tutoring each month.
Health Extension	A demonstrated interest in health care, such as EMT, CPR, or First Aid certification; hospital or clinic work; HIV/AIDS or family planning education or counseling; or lab tech experience.
Hygiene Education/ Sanitation	At least three months (i.e., one summer) of experience in hands-on skilled work, such as mechanical repair, construction, carpentry, or set design.
Agriculture & Forestry Extension	At least three to six months of experience in vegetable gardening, farming, nursery work, tree planting, tree care, or urban forestry.
Youth Development	Six months of full-time work experience with at-risk youth ages 10–25 in a youth-oriented organization.
Community Services	A demonstrated ability in planning, organizing, counseling, or leadership within the past five years. Community services programs are few in number and very competitive; the more experience you have, the stronger your chances will be for a com–munity service assignment.

SOME THINGS TO
KEEP IN MIND

Language

Take at least a year of French or Spanish. The ability to learn a new language is an important ingredient in a successful Peace Corps experience. Many of the programs listed here require at least one year of college-level (or two years high school-level) French or Spanish. Currently, there is a much greater need for French speakers than for Spanish speakers.

Leadership and Community Service

Get involved! Peace Corps service requires commitment and the ability to work well with people. Demonstrated leadership skills are essential qualifying factors in your Peace Corps application, especially for the programs listed here. Taking a leadership role in your community, school, church, or service organization—particularly in planning activities, organizing and motivating groups of people, and project supervision—will strengthen your application.

Medical Information for Applicants

Applicants to the Peace Corps must undergo a comprehensive medical and dental assessment based upon their medical/dental examination and medical history. This will determine if and where they can safely serve in the Peace Corps. If your physician recommends yearly follow-ups for a specific condition, you will be restricted to those countries where the required level of medical support is available. You should be aware of the following information, which may help you determine in advance whether medical/dental assessment of your health will be relatively simple or complex.

Included in Your Peace Corps Application Is a Report of Medical History. Filling out this questionnaire accurately and completely speeds up the medical screening process. Take the time to check your health records so that the health conditions, treatments, and dates you report are correct. *The more accurately you describe health conditions and treatment on the Report of Medical History, the less likely the Peace Corps will need to ask you for more information.* Remember, medical information is confidential and will be forwarded to the Office of Medical Services.

These lists are not inclusive of all conditions that may affect clearance or placement. For further information, you may call the Office of Medical Services, at 1-800-424-8580 ext. 1500 from 9:00 A.M. to 4:00 P.M., Monday through Friday (Eastern time).

If you have any of the following conditions, you will be restricted to those areas of the world that can provide the necessary medical care:

Alcoholism/Substance Addiction, in stable recovery
Allergy to Sulfa Medications
Asthma, mild to moderate
Diabetes
Seizures

With rare exception, the Peace Corps is unable to reasonably accommodate the following conditions:
Addison's Disease
Aneurysm, inoperable
Amyotrophic Lateral Sclerosis (Lou Gehrig's Disease)
Asthma, severe
Cancer of the Bladder
Cancer with Metastasis
Chronic Glomerulonephritis
Chronic Hepatitis
Chronic Obstructive Pulmonary Disease (COPD)
Chronic Pancreatitis
Chronic Pyelonephritis
Chronic Reiter's Syndrome
Claudication
Conditions requiring blood thinner medication
Conditions requiring oral or injectable steroids
Coronary Artery Disease (symptomatic)
Congestive Heart Failure
Connective Tissue Disorder
Diabetes with any complications
Diverticulitis
Endocarditis (heart disease or enlarged heart)
Esophageal Varices
Hemophilia
History of Psychosis
Human Immunodeficiency Virus (HIV)
Inflammatory Bowel Disease
Irreversible Lung Disease (emphysema)
Ischemic Heart Disease
Kidney Stones (recurrent)
Life-threatening allergic reactions
Major Depression (recurrent)
Muscular Dystrophy (progressive)
Myasthenia Gravis
Narcolepsy (poorly controlled)
Optic Neuritis (recurrent)

Osteoporosis with history of stress
fractures
Parkinson's Disease
Pituitary Adenoma with acromegaly
Rheumatoid Arthritis
Sarcoidosis
Symptomatic Cardiac Arrhythmias
Thromobophlebitis, recurrent
Ulcerative Colitis
Ulcerative Proctitis

*If you have any of the following
conditions, your entry into the Peace
Corps will be delayed until resolved:*
Abnormal Pap Smear
Allergies requiring desensitization
injections
Anemia (cause must be identified)
Cataracts requiring surgery
Endometriosis
Gallbladder Disease, including
gallstones
Inguinal Hernia
Internal Hemorrhoids
Kidney or Bladder Infections
Orthodontic Braces
(excluding bite-plate)
Ovarian Cyst
Pilonidal Cyst
Some Psychological Conditions
Uterine Fibroids (symptomatic)

*If you have any of the following condi-
tions, entry into the Peace Corps will be
delayed for at least the time indicated:*
Alcoholism, Substance Addiction—
minimum of two years of
sobriety/abstinence
Cancer—five years cancer-free (three
years for most testicular cancers;
no deferral for most skin cancers
and carcinoma-in-situ)
Coronary artery bypass surgery
or angioplasty—six months
symptom-free, no medications,
normal stress test
Cystic Acne-Accutane treatment—
two months after completion of
therapy
Diabetes—six months well controlled
on oral agents, two years if insulin
dependent, and weight within
recommended range

Eating Disorder—symptom-free
for two years after completion of
therapy
Gastritis, Esophagitis, Peptic or
Duodenal Ulcer—minimum of
six months well controlled,
non-smoker
Glaucoma—three months well controlled with medications or six
months after surgical treatment
Herniated Disc—minimum of two
years symptom-free
Herpes Keratitis (eye)—two years
inactive
High Blood Pressure—three months
well controlled under treatment;
weight within medically recommended range
Joint or Back Disorders must be
stable or mild; weight within
medically recommended range
Joint Replacement (hip, knee, shoulder)—six months post-surgery,
without complications
Kidney Stones (first episode)—one
year
Ligament Reconstruction (knee,
ankle, shoulder) or arthroscopy—
one year
Multiple Sclerosis—minimum of ten
years no exacerbations or new
symptoms
Myocardial Infarction (heart attack)—
twelve months symptom-free, not
on medication, normal stress test
Seizure Disorders—minimum of one
year seizure-free
Stroke—two years symptom-free,
not on medication
20% or more over or 75% or less
than medically recommended
weight for height, with associated
risk factors—until within medically recommended weight, or
risk factors resolved

*Failure to disclose complete
information on your application
can be grounds for administrative
separation from the Peace Corps.*

Revised 10/96

Student Loan Information for Peace Corps Applicants and Volunteers

Volunteers who have outstanding debts under one of the federally administered or guaranteed student load programs qualify for certain relief during their Peace Corps service. The regulations that authorize this relief are sometimes complicated, and different rules apply to different types of loans. This summary of general principles and the following loan-specific descriptions should help you understand the regulations so that you may take advantage of the full range of benefits to which you are entitled.

- When determining the benefits that are available to you, you must consider each type of loan separately (Perkins Loans, Federal Direct Loans, Federal Consolidation Loans, and Stafford Loans [Guaranteed Student Loans or GSLs]). For each type of loan, you must also consider the principal and interest components separately.
- As a Peace Corps volunteer, you do not qualify for loan forgiveness or cancellation unless you have a Perkins Loan. Peace Corps volunteers receive a 15% cancellation of their outstanding Perkins Loan balance for each of their first and second years of service and a 20% cancellation for each of their third and fourth years of service. You do not need to repay loan amounts that are canceled.
- In general, you qualify for deferment of principal payments for all federally administered or guaranteed loans for up to three years.

You do not need to pay amounts deferred during your Peace Corps service, but you generally must resume payments as soon as your service ends. (As of July 1, 1993, Congress consolidated the deferment categories for Direct, Consolidated, and Stafford Loans, subsuming the deferment for Peace Corps volunteers within the broader "economic hardship" category. Some lenders may not be aware of this.)

- The relief from interest payments for which you qualify varies according to the type of loan you have:

  - For Perkins Loans and subsidized Direct Loans, the government will not charge interest while repayment of your principal is deferred (an "abatement of interest").

  - Stafford Loans, Consolidation Loans, and unsubsidized Direct Loans may accrue interest while repayment of the principal is deferred. For these loans, you have two alternatives:

    - For **subsidized** Stafford Loans (and Consolidation Loans that consolidate *only* **subsidized** Stafford Loans) the U.S. Department of Education pays your interest while repayment of the principal is deferred (an "**interest subsidy**").

    - For **unsubsidized** Stafford Loans and **unsubsidized** Direct Loans (and Consolidation Loans that include *any* **unsubsidized** loans) you must make **interest payments** while repayment of your principal is deferred, unless your lender agrees to forbear collection of that interest until a later date.

Forbearance is granted at the discretion of the lender, and it is subject to the lender's terms. Contact your lender for more information.

Perkins Loans
- Volunteers qualify for a 15% loan cancellation for each of their first two years of service and a 20% loan cancellation for their third and fourth years of service. Up to 70% of a Perkins Loan may be canceled.
- Volunteers qualify for a deferment of principal payments and an abatement of interest during their Peace Corps service and for six months immediately after their service ends. For Perkins Loans obtained before July 1, 1993, this relief is limited to three years of Peace Corps service, but for loans obtained on or after that date, it is available for the entire period of a volunteer's service.

Stafford Loans
(Guaranteed Student Loans or GSLs)
- Volunteers qualify for a deferment of principal payments for up to three years during service.
- The U.S. Department of Education pays interest on **subsidized** Stafford Loans during Peace Corps service (an "**interest subsidy**").
- Volunteers with **unsubsidized** Stafford Loans must pay interest during service or apply to their

lender for **forbearance**. The availability and terms of forbearance are entirely at the lender's discretion.

Direct Loans
(William D. Ford Direct Loans)
- Volunteers qualify for a deferment of **principal** payments for up to three years during service.
- The U.S. Department of Education does not charge interest on **subsidized** Direct Loans during Peace Corps service (an "**abatement of interest**").
- Volunteers with **unsubsidized** Direct Loans must pay interest during service or apply to the U.S. Department of Education for **forbearance**.

Consolidation Loans
- Volunteers with Consolidation Loans qualify for a **deferment of principal** payments for up to three years during service.
- The U.S. Department of Education pays interest on Consolidation Loans that consolidate **only subsidized** Stafford Loans (an "**interest subsidy**").
- Volunteers with Consolidation Loans that include **unsubsidized** loans must pay interest during service or apply to their lender for **forbearance**. The availability and terms of forbearance are entirely at the lender's discretion.

Revised 7/15/97

Peace Corps Master's International Program

Graduate School or Peace Corps? Why Not Both?

Many U.S. colleges and universities have graduate programs that are particularly relevant to the challenges that Peace Corps volunteers face overseas. In cooperation with the Peace Corps, selected institutions now offer a compelling route to an advanced degree. As a Master's Internationalist, you can earn your master's degree by completing approximately one year of intensive on-campus study, then serving overseas for two years as a Peace Corps volunteer in a related overseas assignment. These programs are a tremendous benefit to applicants who need additional skills to qualify for Peace Corps programs.

Master's International programs exist in disciplines where there is a skill shortage overseas, so you can be assured that your Peace Corps assignment will make good use of your skills. Serving in one of ninety-one countries which host the Peace Corps, you will almost certainly have greater responsibilities than your stateside peers. Through this innovative program, you will build your qualifications while helping people overseas help themselves.

What sets Master's International students apart from traditional master's students?
As a Master's International student, you not only get two years of valuable, international work experience; you also receive up to 12 credits toward those required to graduate. Some institutions even offer financial assistance to Master's International students.

In some programs, your work overseas counts as the field practicum required for the degree. Other universities may require the compilation of a diary during overseas duty. Still others will ask you to complete a paper or an additional semester of coursework upon your return to the U.S.

What are the eligibility requirements?
University requirements vary but most programs require a bachelor's degree from an accredited college, and Graduate Record Examination scores. To qualify for the Peace Corps you must be a U.S. citizen and at least 18 years of age. There is no upper age limit. Of course, in addition to these basic requirements, you must have a skill that is in demand overseas. You cannot have any legal encumbrances, and you must pass rigorous medical screening. Married couples are more difficult to place since both husband and wife must have assignments in a single locale.

How does it work?
You will need to submit applications simultaneously to the university and to the Peace Corps. **This must take place at least six months prior to the beginning of the academic year in which you will enroll.** The Peace Corps and the academic institution will consider your applications separately and accept you into the program jointly.

With the application to the Peace Corps, you must submit a **letter of intent** that states the following:
- To which MI school you have applied or intend to apply
- If you are applying to more than one school, which school is your first choice
- The title of the degree you are pursuing. If appropriate, include

any additional areas of specialization you will pursue within the degree area
- When you expect to begin classes
- When you expect to complete your academic work prior to Peace Corps service.

Applying early to the program should allow enough time for you to receive the necessary medical, legal, and suitability clearances prior to beginning the program. After this portion of the application process is completed, you will receive preliminary clearance for Peace Corps service contingent on the completion of the academic course requirements.

Please note that while you will begin the program about a year before going overseas, you will not receive your specific job and country assignment until after your application has gone through all the necessary clearances. Once the application has been cleared and sent to the appropriate skill desk, **you should receive an invitation to a Peace Corps project approximately three to six months prior to your departure overseas.** This is particularly important to keep in mind if you are required to plan a research study prior to your departure.

For more information about enrolling in a Master's International Program, contact your local recruitment office (1-800-424-8580, option 1) OR Office of University Programs Peace Corps Headquarters 1111 20th St., NW Washington, D.C. 20526 202-606-9322 or 800-424-8580, option 2, ext. 2226.

The universities participating in the program in various fields are listed as follows:

AGRICULTURE AND FORESTRY

Arizona State University, East
Program: Agribusiness
Founded Summer 1998
Admissions Deadlines—
    No specific dates
Admissions Cycle—Rolling
Program Start—Fall; Spring

Description—The School of Agribusiness and Resource Management and the Center for Agribusiness Policy offers a Master of Science degree in Agribusiness. The Master's International program consists of 33 credits, 6 of which may be earned for Peace Corps volunteer service. The program is designed to prepare student participants for assignments in agribusiness management and for volunteer and development activities generally. Courses will cover issues such as advanced agribusiness marketing, management and finance, food management, international agricultural techniques, world agricultural development, and advanced agribusiness policy. Depending on the nature of their assignment or their particular interests, students will register for internship, independent study, and/or research credits.

Requirements—3.0 minimum GPA for undergraduate college studies; no GRE scores required.

Benefits—Students may earn up to six credits for the Peace Corps volunteer service.

Contact—Julie Stanton, Assistant Professor, Morrison School of Agribusiness and Resource Mngt., ASU East—Mail Code 0180, 6001 S. Power Road, AGB 2-107, Mesa, AZ 85206-0180. Telephone: (602) 727-1126; Fax: (602) 727-1011; E-mail: jstanton@asu.edu.

Cornell University
Program: International Agriculture
Founded Fall 1997
Admissions Deadline—Rolling
Admissions Cycle—Rolling
Program Start—Fall

Description—The Master of Professional Studies/Agriculture program has an emphasis on conservation of natural resources, sustainable farming systems, and various aspects of international development such as population, nutrition, planning, policy, or agriculture. The program prepares students, through a combination of academic studies and application of analytical skills, to assume a leadership position in development programs, in government and nongovernment organizations, or in the private sector. The MPS/A combined with a Peace Corps tour will require satisfactory completion of 30 units of academic study prior to Peace Corps service. Students can opt for either the 9–15 credit thesis tract or the 3–9 credit project report tract. The project report consists of a written independent study report describing the student's volunteer assignment and demonstrates how the civil/environmental engineering profession was utilized in this project. In addition, students are required to take courses derived from the areas of civil/environmental engineering, project management/leadership/consensus building/environmental policy, and environmental microbiology/public health biology. The remainder of the coursework consists of a minimum of 18 credits of technical electives.

Requirements—(1) A baccalaureate degree granted by a university of recognized standing, or completion of studies equivalent to those required for a baccalaureate degree at Cornell; (2) evidence of ability to perform well in graduate studies at Cornell, such as undergraduate academic record, Graduate Record Exam scores, and letters of recommendation; (3) a statement of purpose projecting clear professional objectives that could be well served by the joint MPS/Peace Corps program at Cornell.

Benefits—During Peace Corps service, students are not required to pay full tuition. They will, however, be required to pay an absentia tuition of $200 per semester. Up to 6 credit hours may be earned in the Peace Corps through the completion and acceptance of the MPS project paper.

Contact—Dr. James Haldeman, Box 14 Kennedy Hall, Cornell University, Ithaca, NY 14853. Telephone: (607) 255-3037; Fax: (607) 255-1005; E-mail: JEH@cornell.edu.

Florida International University
Program: Forestry/Environmental
  Education
Founded Spring 1998
Admissions Deadlines—Fall/March
  15; Spring/October 15
Admissions Cycle—Rolling
Program Start—Fall; Spring

Description—The Department of Environmental Studies, College of Arts and Sciences offers a Master of Science degree in environmental studies with a concentration in biological management. The program is designed to prepare student participants in areas of forestry, agroforestry, and environmental education, and for volunteer and development activities generally. The MIP consists of a minimum of 36 semester units of academic study, in which 20 of the units are expected to be completed before students begin their Peace Corps assignments. Courses will cover issues such as restoration ecology, sustainable development, environmental resource policy, environment and development, tropical forest conservation, and protected area management.

Requirements—GRE scores of 1000 or higher; minimum 3.0 GPA; three letters of recommendation; and a short (one- to two-page) statement of research interests and intent.

Benefits—Students may earn up to 6 credits for their Peace Corps volunteer service.

Contact—Mahadev Bhat, Graduate Studies Program, Florida International University, University Park, ECS 333, Miami, FL 33199. Telephone: (305) 348-1210; E-mail: bhatm@fiu.edu; Website: www.fiu.edu/~envstud.
OR
Farley Ferrante, Peace Corps Coordinator; Phone: (305) 348-3641; Fax: (305) 348-2721; E-mail: fferra01@fiu.edu.

North Carolina State University
Program: Forest/Natural Resources
Founded Summer 1998
Admissions Deadlines—Fall/June 25; Spring/Nov. 25; Summer/March 25
Admissions Cycle—Rolling
Program Start—Fall Semester

Description—Graduate students enrolled in the College of Forest Resources, Department of Forestry will be able to pursue a Master of Forestry, Master of Natural Resources, or a Master of Science degree in Forestry or Natural Resources. The MIP will consist of a minimum of 36 semester hours of academic study for the Master of Natural Resources or the Master of Forestry, or 30 semester hours of academic study for the Master

of Science. The program is designed to prepare students for Peace Corps assignments in forestry (primarily agroforestry) and/or natural resources management with an emphasis on environmental education, and for volunteer and development activities generally. Students will develop a course of study in consultation with their advisor and their faculty advisory committee.

Requirements—3.0 minimum GPA; GRE scores; completion of recommendation form (or letter) from three references; statement of professional/research objectives; two official copies of all college-level transcripts. A resume of all relevant experience is frequently helpful but not required. Admission requires departmental acceptance, with at least one member of the faculty volunteering in advance to serve as an advisor.

Benefits—Each of the three degree programs will include 6 units of independent study related to the students' Peace Corps volunteer service. Research assistantships are available on a competitive basis to students pursuing research-based Master of Science degrees.

Contact—Erin Sills, Department of Forestry, Box 8008, North Carolina State University, Raleigh, NC 27695. Telephone: (919) 515-7784; Fax: (919) 515-6193; E-mail: sills@cfr.cfr.ncsu.edu.

Purdue University
The Purdue University MI Program in Agriculture is now offering the Master of Science degree in Entomology with both a thesis or non-thesis option
Note: This program is currently under review. Please contact Purdue for further information.

Santa Clara University
Program: Agribusiness
Founded Winter 1998
Admissions Deadlines—
 March 1 (early Fall), June 1 (Fall),
 September 1 (Winter), December 1
 (Spring)
Admissions Cycle—Rolling
Program Start—Fall, Winter, or
 Spring quarters

Description—The Leavey School of
Business and Administration at Santa
Clara University offers a Master of
Business Administration (MBA) with
a specialization in agribusiness. The
program is designed to prepare students for careers in the food and agribusiness industry and to contribute
to more effective volunteer service in
the scarce skill areas of agriculture
economics/farm management and
advanced business development.
Depending on the coursework
already completed by the student
prior to admission, the agribusiness
MBA program requires a minimum of
fifteen courses (45 quarter units) and
a maximum of twenty-four courses
(72 quarter units). The on-campus
coursework is complemented by
three enrichment programs: a mentor
program, internships, and international study tours. The Leavey School
of Business at Santa Clara University
is the only nationally ranked business
school that offers a degree in agribusiness management.

Requirements—Applicants must
have a bachelor's degree in any field,
an official GMAT score, and a complete Leavey School of Business
application for admission.

Benefits—Full and partial scholarships are available through the Institute of Agribusiness. Assistantships
and loans are available through the
university. Students can earn six (6)
quarter units for their Peace Corps
service through two consecutive

internships or through an internship
followed by an independent study.
Participants will work with their
advisors to determine the best course
of study.

Contact—S. Andrew Starbird, Ph.D.,
Director, Food & Agribusiness
Institute, Leavey School of Business
Administration, Santa Clara Univer-
sity, Santa Clara, CA 95053. Tele-
phone: (408) 554-4086; Fax: (408)
554-5167; E-mail: fai@scu.edu;
Website: http://lsb.scu.edu/fai.

The University of New Mexico
Program: Environmental
 Education/Parks and Recreation
Founded Fall 1997
Admissions Deadlines—
 November 17, April 17, June 17
Admissions Cycles—Rolling
Program Start—Spring, Summer, Fall

Description—The University of
New Mexico College of Education
offers a Master of Arts in Parks and
Recreation with an emphasis in
either Environmental Education or
Parks and Recreation Administration. The program is designed to
prepare students for Peace Corps
assignments in parks, recreation,
and environmental education, and
for volunteer and development
activities generally. The students will
receive one year (three semesters) of
academic preparation in their field
of study before entering service as
Peace Corps volunteers. The program consists of a minimum of 45
semester units of academic study.
Courses will cover issues such as
multicultural environmental education, organization and administration
of parks and recreation agencies,
community relations, leadership
development, and urban and rural
natural resources planning. Both
emphasis areas require completed
comprehensive examinations prior
to the start of Peace Corps service.

Minority participation in the program is encouraged.

Requirements—Bachelor's degree with major in parks, recreation, leisure studies, environmental education, or a related field; a minimum GPA of 3.0; three letters of recommendation; a letter of intent and statement of career goals and areas of experience and/or interests; history of student's academic and professional background; GREs optional.

Benefits—The Peace Corps will fulfill the Advanced Field Experience requirements in which students may earn 12 credits from the university.

Contact—Paul S. Miko, Ph.D., College of Education, University of New Mexico, Johnson Center, 112C, Albuquerque, NM 87131-1251. Telephone: (505) 277-8172; Fax: (505) 277-6227; E-mail: pmiko@unm.edu.

BUSINESS

Monterey Institute of International Studies (MIIS)
The Graduate School of International Management (GSIM) at MIIS offers an International Master of Business Administration degree that prepares Peace Corps volunteers for international business development.
Contact: Nancy Trevino, Academic Programs Associate, Fisher Graduate School of International Business, Monterey Institute of International Studies, 425 Van Buren Street, Monterey, CA 93940. Telephone: (408) 647-6586; Fax: (408) 647-6506; E-mail: ntrevino@miis.edu.

University of the Pacific
Program: Business
Founded Spring 1997
Admissions Deadlines—Fall/July 1, though it is recommended that students applying for financial aid submit their applications by March 31
Admissions Cycle—Rolling
Program Start—Fall, Spring, or Summer

Description—The Eberhardt School of Business offers a Master of Business Administration (MBA) degree in conjunction with the Peace Corps. The program is designed to prepare students for their service as business development volunteers. Peace Corps service fulfills the internship requirement for the degree. The university offers both a standard and an accelerated MBA curriculum. The standard curriculum requires 54 semester units, while the accelerated curriculum requires students to complete a minimum of 30 semester units for the degree. Students spend either one or two semesters on campus before Peace Corps service and return for a final semester to complete their coursework.

Requirements—Bachelor's degree in any field; GMAT scores; applications are considered on the basis of GPA and work experience where applicable.

Benefits—MI students can apply their Peace Corps service toward the completion of the degree program's internship requirements; for each semester following their Peace Corps service, students are forgiven one-third of their tuition costs for a graduate assistantship.

Contact—Dr. Newman Peery, MBA Program Director, Eberhardt School of Business, University of the Pacific, 3601 Pacific Avenue, Stockton, CA 95211. Telephone: (209) 946-2642; Fax: (209) 946-2586; E-mail: npeery@uop.edu.

ENGINEERING

Michigan Technological University
Program: Civil and Environmental
  Engineering
Founded Spring 1997
Admissions Deadlines—No specific
  deadlines, though students should
  submit applications at least 6
  months prior to the beginning
  of the fall quarter
Admissions Cycle—Once per year
Program Start—Fall

Description—MTU offers a Master of
Science (MS) in Civil Engineering
and MS in Environmental Engineering. The degree requires 3 quarters of
coursework totaling 45 quarter units
of academic study prior to Peace
Corps service. Students can opt for
either the 9–15 credit thesis tract or
the 3–9 credit project report tract.
The project report consists of a
written independent study report
describing the student's volunteer
assignment and demonstrates how
the civil/environmental engineering
profession was utilized in this
project. In addition, students are
required to take courses derived
from the areas of civil/environmental
engineering, project management/
leadership/consensus building/envi-
ronmental policy, and environmental
microbiology/public health biology.
The remainder of the coursework
consists of a minimum of 18 credits
of technical electives. Home Page:
http://bigmac.civil.mtu.edu/pub-
lic_html/KGP/peacecorp.html

Requirements—ABET-accredited
bachelor's degree in engineering;
minimum 3.0 GPA recommended.

Benefits—Student can earn up to
9 credits of independent study for
Peace Corps service; tuition costs
for credits earned through Peace
Corps service are waived, graduate

teaching assistantships and positions
as hourly graders are available.

Contact—Dr. James Mihelcic, Associate Professor, Civil & Environmental Engineering, Michigan Techno-
logical University, 1400 Townsend
Drive, Houghton, MI 49931-1295.
Telephone: (906) 487-2334; Fax:
(906) 487-3292; E-mail:
jm41@mtu.edu.

NONPROFIT MANAGEMENT

Illinois State University
Program: Nonprofit
Management/Community
  Development
Founded Fall 1997
Admissions Deadlines—No specific
  deadlines, rolling admissions
Admissions Cycle—Rolling
Program Start—Fall and Spring

Description—Illinois State University offers a Nonprofit Management/
Community Development concentration in the Master's program in
Political Science. Students are
trained to meet the Peace Corps'
need for volunteers with scarce skills
in Community Service Administration and Nonprofit/NGO Management. Master's International Students
complete twelve to eighteen months
of study, including the applied-focus
core courses shared by the existing
ISU Peace Corps Fellows Program in
Applied Community and Economic
Development.

Requirements—A demonstrated
interest in community development;
a two-page statement of purpose;
completed graduate school and
assistantship applications; two official undergraduate transcripts; GRE
scores for some programs; and three
letters of recommendation, at least
one from a person familiar with
applicant's academic work.

Benefits—Master's International students may apply Peace Corps service toward completion of the degree's internship requirement. Tuition and fees are waived during Peace Corps service.

Contact—Michael Kelleher, Director, Department of Economics, Box 4200, Illinois State University, Normal, Illinois 61790-4200. Phone: (309) 438-8685; Fax: (309) 438-5228; E-mail: fmkelle@ilstu.edu; Website: http://www.econ.ilstu.edu/PeaceCorps/PCorps.html.

School for International Training
Program: Nonprofit Management and NGO Development
Founded Spring 1997
Admissions Deadlines—No specific deadlines, though it is recommended that applications be received by April 1
Admissions Cycle—Rolling
Program Start—Fall

Description—The School for International Training (SIT) awards a Master of International and Intercultural Management through the Program in Intercultural Management (PIM). Coursework in sustainable development, human resource development and training, and international education or a combination of these fields will provide the necessary knowledge and skills for work with NGOs (nongovernmental organizations) in diverse settings. PIM emphasizes the development of intercultural competencies through coursework that is experiential, practical, and participatory. This foundation ensures that students succeed in their Peace Corps experience. The program has three phases: a nine-month on-campus component, Peace Corps service where the relationship between theory and practice is assessed, and a

two-week Capstone Seminar and research paper. Students must also meet a language requirement before graduation.

Requirements—Bachelor's degree or equivalent; professional and intercultural experience; ability to analyze experience and utilize it as a source of learning.

Benefits—Peace Corps service fulfills the professional practicum requirement; students are not charged tuition or fees while they serve as Peace Corps volunteers; SIT grant, work-study, scholarships, and federal loans are available; financial aid application priority deadline is April 1.

Contact—Admissions Office, SIT, Box 676, Brattleboro, VT 05302. Telephone: (800) 336-1616 or (802) 258-3267; Fax: (802) 258-3500; E-mail: admissions@sit.edu; Website: www.sit.edu.

PUBLIC HEALTH AND NUTRITION

Boston University
Offers a Master's in Public Health (MPH). Contact: Lisa Bilgen de Herrera, Director of Marketing and Intercultural Programs, 715 Albany Street, T4W, Boston, MA 02118-2526. Telephone: (617) 638-5234; Fax: (617) 638-4476; E-mail: lherrera@bu.edu.

Emory University
Program: Public Health
Founded Fall 1998
Admissions Deadline—
February 1 (for school scholarship consideration); February 15 (for all other applications)
Admissions Cycle—Once per year
Program Start—Fall

Description—The Rollins School of Public Health offers a Master of Public Health degree in conjunction with the Peace Corps' Master's International Program. Graduate students enrolled at Emory will be required to complete 42 semester units of academic study toward their MPH. The MIPPH will award 3 credits toward the thesis/special study requirement for the MPH degree at RSPH contingent upon successful completion of overseas services as a Peace Corps volunteer. Tuition and fees will be waived from the three (3) credit-hour requirement. While students are overseas, they will be expected to submit quarterly activity/research reports. The program is designed to improve MIPPH Peace Corps volunteers' ability to make positive, sustainable contributions to improving the health and well-being of the communities in which they serve.

Requirements—Bachelor's degree from an accredited college or university; GRE scores (applicants with doctoral-level degrees are exempt from taking the GRE); two letters of recommendation; and a statement of purpose. International applicants are required to take the Test of English as a Foreign Language (TOEFL).

Benefits—Tuition and fees will be waived for the 3 credit-hour thesis/special study requirement. Financial aid is available on a competitive basis.

Contact—For a complete application packet and catalog, send your name and address to dmit@sph.emory.edu. You may also contact James C. Setzer, Senior Associate/Program Coordinator, Department of International Health, The Rollins School of Public Health, Emory University, 1518 Clifton Rd., NE, Atlanta, GA 30322. Telephone: (404) 727-3338;

Fax: (404) 727-4590; E-mail: setzer@sph.emory.edu
OR
Shannon Shelton, Assistant Director for Academic Programs, Department of International Health, The Rollins School for Public Health, Emory University, 1518 Clifton Rd., NE, Atlanta, GA 30322. Phone: (404) 727-3338; Fax: (404) 727-4590; E-mail: sshel01@sph.emory.edu.

George Washington University
The Department of Health Care Sciences hosts a Master's of Public Health program (MPH) which offers several tracks of special interest including health promotion/disease prevention and international health. Contact: Eric Madsen, Administrative Officer, The GW Center for International Health, Ross Hall 125, 2300 I Street, NW, Washington, DC 20037. Telephone: (202) 994-4473; Fax: (202) 994-0900; E-mail: iphjem@gwumc.edu.

University of North Carolina at Chapel Hill
The School of Public Health (SPH) offers master's degrees in maternal and child health, nutrition, nursing, and health administration. Contact: Deborah Bender, Research Associate Professor and MI Program Coordinator, Department of Health Policy and Administration, School of Public Health, University of North Carolina at Chapel Hill, Chapel Hill, NC 27599-7400. Telephone: (919) 966-7383; E-mail: deborahbender@unc.edu.

TEACHING ENGLISH AS A SECOND LANGUAGE

American University

Program: TESOL
Founded Fall 1998
Admissions Deadline—Rolling
Admissions Cycle—Rolling
Program Start—Fall

Description—The Master's International Program enables participants to qualify for Peace Corps TEFL assignments through graduate coursework leading to an MA in TESOL. MIP/MA TESOL participants can qualify for Peace Corps assignments in Secondary School TESOL Instruction, University English Teaching, and University-Level English Teacher Training. At the completion of the program, participants are ready to enter the job market with excellent academic credentials and significant overseas teaching experience. MIP/MA TESOL students who successfully complete their Peace Corps service earn, at no cost, 6 credits of cooperative education field experience. In addition, they are waived from the 3-credit TESOL practicum course based on their Peace Corps teaching experience.

Requirements—Bachelor's degree from an accredited college or university with a 3.0 GPA, two letters of recommendation, a written statement of purpose, and American University's standard graduate application. No prior study of linguistics or teaching experience required, but it is recommended that native English speakers have at least one other language than English.

Benefits—6 credits are earned for the cooperative education field experience; tuition is waived for these 6 credits during Peace Corps service.

Contact—TESOL Program, Department of Language and Foreign Studies, American University, 4400 Massachusetts Ave., NW, Washington, DC 20016-1076. Telephone: (202) 885-1076; Fax: (202) 885-1076; E-mail: tesol@american.edu; Website: www.american.edu/tesol.

California State University at Sacramento

The Department of English offers a Master of Arts in Teaching English to Speakers of Other Languages (TESOL).
Contact: Dr. Linda Callis Buckley, TESOL Coordinator, English Department, 6000 J Street, Sacramento, CA 95819-6075. Telephone: (916) 278-6586; Fax: (916) 278-5410; E-mail: buckleyl@saclink.csus.edu.

Colorado State University

Program: TESOL
Founded Fall 1998
Admissions Deadline—
    Fall/February; Spring/July;
    no summer admissions
Program Start—Fall or Spring

Description—The Department of English in the College of Liberal Arts offers a Master of English with a concentration in Teaching English to Speakers of Other Languages (TESOL). The program consists of 33 to 35 credits of academic work, in which the student is required to complete 16 to 18 credits before beginning Peace Corps service. The TESOL concentration will prepare student-volunteers for assignments in university English teaching and English teacher training. The degree program is quite general in that it does not focus on a particular type of English language teaching which gives students flexibility in developing their own teaching style. Peace Corps service may be used to fulfill the internship requirement, to use as the basis for a final project or thesis, or it may be used to meet both requirements. After service, students will return to CSU to complete the remainder of their required coursework.

Requirements—Bachelor's degree in any field with a minimum 3.0 GPA, letters of recommendation, and GRE scores.

Benefits—Peace Corps service can be used to fulfill the internship requirement, the basis for a final project, or both.

Contact—Carol Cantrell, Graduate Coordinator, Department of English, Colorado State University, 359 Eddy, Ft. Collins, CO 80523-1773. Telephone: (970) 491-6428; E-mail: ccantrell@vines.colostate.edu; Website: www.colostate.edu/Depts/English/english_ie4.htm

URBAN PLANNING

Virginia Polytechnic Institute and State University
Program: Urban and Regional Development
Founded Spring 1998
Admissions Deadline—Rolling, March 1 for financial aid requests
Admissions Cycle—None
Program Start—August 15

Description—The College of Architecture and Urban Studies offers a Master of Urban and Regional Planning and a Master of Urban Affairs degree in conjunction with the Peace Corps. The program is designed to prepare students for their service as urban development volunteers. Courses cover such subjects as community and economic development, public budgeting and management, international development policy and planning, natural resources planning, pollution control, land use and environmental planning, community renewable energy systems, and urban growth management. Students may also select courses involving rural development, environmental planning, and regional development. Before beginning their Peace Corps assignments, student participants will be expected to have made satisfactory progress toward their degree. The students' Peace Corps service may provide a foundation for a thesis or major paper as determined by students and their faculty advisors. Minority participation is encouraged.

Requirements—Bachelor's degree from accredited college or university.

Benefits—Students can earn 2–6 credits for a practicum, thesis, or major paper based on their Peace Corps service.

Contact—John Randolph, Chair, Department of Urban Affairs and Planning, 201 Architecture Annex, Virginia Tech, Blacksburg, VA 24061-0113. Telephone: (540) 231-6971; Fax: (540) 231-3367; E-mail: uapvt@vt.edu; Website: www.arch.vt.edu/caus/ua/uapintro.html.

Alternative Organizations

Alliances Abroad
409 Deep Eddy Avenue
Austin, TX 78703
(512) 457-8062
http://www.alliancesabroad.com
Alliances Abroad's program allows participants to experience the culture of another country through volunteer work that lasts anywhere from six weeks to one year. Alliances Abroad offers programs in sixteen countries and strives to offer full service, such as travel arrangements, country information, local support, and reminder service. A cost is involved. This is not a free program.

American Red Cross
National Office of Volunteers
Division of Youth Involvement
8111 Gatehouse Road, 2nd Floor
Falls Church, VA 22042
(703) 206-8375
http://www.redcross.org
The American Red Cross is a humanitarian organization, led by volunteers, that provides relief to victims of disasters and helps people prevent, prepare for, and respond to emergencies. To do this work, the Red Cross needs the help of people of all ages, both in the U.S. and around the world. Among the areas in which it provides help are disaster; service to members of the armed forces; health and safety, including HIV/AIDS education; international; and youth involvement. Call your local Red Cross to learn about educational and training and volunteer and community services opportunities.

AmeriCorps or AmeriCorps VISTA
Please see Corporation for National Service.

Amigos de las Americas
5618 Star Lane
Houston, TX   77057
(713) 782-5290 or (800) 231-7796
http://www.amigoslink.org
Amigos sends approximately 500 volunteers a year to countries in Latin America for terms of one to two months. Programs are centered around public health and community development projects.

Citizens Democracy Corps
1400 I Street, NW Suite 1125
Washington, DC 20005
(202) 872-0933 or (800) 394-1945
CDC operates a national Volunteer Registry which refers individuals to over eighty organizations with programs in the region, as well as two volunteer programs of its own: Business Entrepreneur Program (provides on-site technical assistance to small and midsized companies in the region by enlisting the expertise of U.S. businesspersons with entrepreneurial skills) and CDC-Sponsored Volunteer Program (supports a number of targeted volunteer projects in diverse sectors which address local needs).

Club TELI
Dominique Girerd
clubteli@cyberaccess.fr
This nonprofit organization offers interesting alternatives for those wishing to go abroad to study, work, or start a career. Distributes a free monthly publication listing opportunities abroad to their members.

Corporation for National Service
1201 New York Avenue, NW
Washington, DC 20525
(800) 942-2677
http://www.cns.gov
CNS is the umbrella organization for AmeriCorps, AmeriCorps VISTA, the Senior Corps, and Learn and Serve America. These government-sponsored volunteer programs are

each diverse and domestically oriented. See their website or call for more information.

CUSO
2255 Carling Avenue, Suite 400
Ottawa, Ontario
CANADA K2B 1A6
(613) 829-7445
cusoppu@web.net

Limited to citizens or permanent residents of Canada. CUSO offers two-year assignments in Africa, Asia, Latin America, the Caribbean and the Pacific. All volunteers must be skilled in their assignment area; college training is required for some placements. CUSO recruits Canadian citizens for the United Nations Volunteer Program as well. All expenses are covered.

Earthwatch
680 Mount Auburn Street
Watertown, MA 02172
(617) 926—8200 or (800) 776-0188
http://www.earthwatch.org

Earthwatch is a twenty-year-old nonprofit charity that allows volunteers, eighteen years and older, to participate on peer-reviewed scientific conservation projects/field research around the planet for two to three weeks.

Global Volunteers
375 East Little Canada Road
St. Paul, MN 55117
(612) 482-1074 or (800) 487-1074
http://www.globalvlntrs.org

GV is a private, nonprofit U.S. corporation founded with the goal of helping to establish a foundation for peace through mutual international understanding. Its programs center around a one-, two- or three-week volunteer experience in Southeast Asia, Africa, Latin America, the Caribbean, Europe, or the U.S. where teams of volunteers live and work with local people on human and economic development projects.

Habitat for Humanity, International
322 West Lamar Street
Americus, GA 31709
(912) 924-6935 or (800) HABITAT
http://www.habitat.org

Habitat is an ecumenical, Christian-based, nonprofit organization dedicated to eliminating the effects of poverty through the construction of inexpensive, quality housing. Skilled and nonskilled persons are welcome. Terms of service last approximately three years.

Institute for International Cooperation and Development
P.O. Box 103-H
Williamstown, MA 01267
(413) 458-9828
http://www.berkshire.net/~iicdl

IICD is a nonprofit, educational organization founded in 1986 and dedicated to promoting global understanding and international solidarity through programs to countries in Africa and Latin America. The programs are six to twenty months long and include preparation and follow-up periods at the Institute in Massachusetts.

International Volunteers Program
Council on International
    Educational Exchange
205 East 42nd Street
New York, NY 10017
(212) 661-1414 or (888) COUNCIL
http://www.ciee.org

IVP is a nonprofit, nongovernmental, educational organization founded in 1947 with the mission of developing educational exchanges and fostering international understanding. Today, with programs in thirty-four countries, it offers a wide range of international programs and services for students, faculty, and the general public. A cost is involved. This is not a free program.

International Volunteers for Peace
SCI-IVS USA
Innisfree Village, Route 2
P.O. Box 506C
Crozet, VA 22932
　　IVP is an international network
of organizations that organizes work
camps, typically from two to four
weeks in duration.

Learn and Serve America
See Corporation for National Service.

**U.S. Agency for International
Development**
Recruitment Branch
1550 Wilson Boulevard, Room 658A
SA-36
Washington, DC 20523-3607
Student Programs: (703) 302-4071
http://www.usaid.gov
　　The United States Agency for
International Development (USAID)
is the independent government
agency that provides economic
development and humanitarian
assistance to advance U.S. economic
and political interests overseas.

Visions in Action
2710 Ontario Rd., NW
Washington, DC 20009
(202) 625-7402
http://www.igc.org/visions
　　Visions in Action sends volunteers
to Africa and Latin America to work
for indigenous nonprofits and the
media in a variety of sectors, including human rights, journalism, health,
environment, social work, and community development. Volunteers
cover their own costs for six- or
twelve-month placements.

VISTA or AmeriCorps VISTA
Please see Corporation for National
Service.

Voluntary Service Overseas
317 Putney Bridge Road
London SW15 2PN
England
011-081-780-2266
　　VSO is a group that places volunteers from all walks of life, on one of
many two-year projects in a developing nation. The aim of VSO projects
is to "help people help themselves."

Volunteers Exchange International
134 West 26th Street
New York, NY 10001
(212) 206-7307
http://www.igc.apc.org/vei
　　VEI is a member committee of an
international network of volunteers:
The Federation of the International
Christian Youth Exchange (ICYE).
VEI is a nonprofit organization that
promotes international understanding and sensitivity to social, political,
and economic realities in the world
through work camps and exchange
programs for young people aged
eighteen to thirty. A cost is involved.
This is not a free program.

Volunteers for Peace, Inc.
43 Tiffany Road
Belmont, VT 05730-0202
(800) 259-2759
http://www.vfp.org
　　VFP is an international volunteer
work camp organization and has been
organizing programs worldwide since
1981. The programs aim to promote
citizen diplomacy by maximizing
personal contact with local people.

Volunteers in Asia, Inc.
P.O. Box 4543
Stanford, CA 94301
(415) 723-3228
　　Volunteers in Asia, Inc. sends
volunteers to Asia to teach English
and to work on community development. Their volunteer program is
structured similar to that of the
Peace Corps.

Volunteers in Overseas Cooperative Assistance
50 F Street, NW Suite 1075
Washington, DC 20001
(202) 383-4961 or (800) 929-8622

VOCA is an organization that sends volunteers overseas for two weeks to three months to perform agricultural development, as well as small and medium business development, in developing countries.

World Relief
P.O. Box WRC
Wheaton, IL 60189
(708) 665-0236 or (800) 535-5433

World Relief offers one- and two-year assignments through its Open Hands program in Africa, Latin America, Asia, and the Pacific. Volunteers must be Christian and active in a local church. A college degree and/or language skills are usually required. Couples with dependents are sometimes accepted. Expenses are not always covered. In some cases the volunteers are responsible for travel and part of their living expenses.

WorldTeach
Harvard Institute on
International Development
One Eliott Street
Cambridge, MA 02138
(617) 495-5527 or
(800) 4-TEACH-O
http://www.hiid.harvard.edu

WorldTeach is sponsored through Harvard University. It sends 250 volunteers around the world—Africa, Eastern Europe, Central & South America, and Asia—to teach English. In Africa, some math and science courses may be taught. A small stipend is given to each volunteer, per month, out of the program fee which is paid to the university.

Note: The philosophies, practices, and views of these organizations are not, in whole or in part, the official views of the Peace Corps and/or the government of the United States. The information listed above is for reference purposes only.

Peace Corps Regional Offices

Atlanta
(AL, FL, GA, MS, PR, SC, TN)
Maisha Strozier, Mgr.
Acting: Eric Florimon-Reed
and Stephanie Greene
100 Alabama Street
Building 1924, Suite 2R70
Atlanta, GA 30303
(404) 562-3456/3472
Fax: (404) 562-3455

Boston
(MA, ME, NH, RI, VT)
Jean Siegle, Mgr.
Rae Mims, PAS
10 Causeway Street
Room 450
Boston, MA 02222
(617) 565-5555/5541
Fax: (617) 565-5539

Chicago
(IL, IN, KY, MI, MO, OH)
Kim Mansaray, Mgr.
Carol Wilkerson, PAS
Xerox Center
55 West Monroe Street
Suite 450
Chicago, IL 60603
(312) 353-4990/7716
Fax: (312) 353-4192

Chicago Admin.
Mark Pusinelli, Admin. Off.
Robert Logan, Asst. AO
Xerox Center
55 West Monroe Street
Suite 450
Chicago, IL 60603
(312) 353-7963
Fax: (312) 353-4192

Dallas
(AR, LA, NM, OK, TX)
Morris Baker, Mgr.
Laurene Wistner, PAS
207 South Houston Street
Room 257
Dallas, TX 75202
(214) 767-5435/5438
Fax: (214) 767-5483

Denver
(CO, KS, NE, UT, WY)
Karen Nakandakare, Mgr.
Jeff Martin, PAS
1999 Broadway
Suite 2205
Denver, CO 80202-3050
(303) 844-7020/7017
Fax: (303) 844-7010

Los Angeles
(AZ, Southern CA)
John Hartley, Mgr.
TBD, PAS
11000 Wilshire Blvd.
Suite 8104
Los Angeles, CA 90024
(310) 235-7444
Fax: (310) 235-7442

Minneapolis
(IA, MN, ND, SD, WI)
David Belina, Mgr.
Kevin Burns, PAS
330 2nd Avenue South
Suite 420
Minneapolis, MN 55401
(612) 348-1480/1483
Fax: (612) 348-1474

New York
(CT, NJ, NY, PA)
John Coyne, Mgr.
Adrienne Berman, PAS
6 World Trade Center
Room 611
New York, NY 10048
(212) 637-6498/6495
Fax: (212) 637-6494

Rosslyn
(DC, DE, MD, NC, VA, WV)
Monica Mills, Mgr.
Felisa Neuringer, PAS
1400 Wilson Blvd.
Suite 400
Arlington, VA 22209
(703) 235-9191/97/99
Fax: (703) 235-9189

San Francisco
(Northern CA, HI, NV)
Harris Bostic, Mgr.
Heidi Thoren, PAS
333 Market Street
Suite 600
San Francisco, CA 94105
(415) 977-8800/8786
Fax: (415) 977-8803

Seattle
(AK, ID, MT, OR, WA)
Dorothy Culjat, Mgr.
Carla Semmler, PAS
2001 Sixth Ave., Suite 1776
Seattle, WA 98121
(206) 553-5490/8434
Fax: (206) 553-2343

Revised 7/24/98

Returned Peace Corps Volunteer Groups

National Peace Corps Association (NPCA)
1900 L Street, NW, Suite 205
Washington, DC 20036-5002
(202) 293-RPCV

**LOCAL RPCV GROUPS
(Listed alphabetically by state):**

Birmingham Area RPCVs
2918 Rhodes Circle, Apt. 1
Birmingham, AL 35205
(205) 933-5399

Alaska RPCVs
P.O. Box 241324
Anchorage, AK 99524-1324

Phoenix RPCVs
P.O. Box 32438
Phoenix, AZ 85064-2428
(602) 253-2019

RPCVs of Southern Arizona
Box 501, Education Building
University of Arizona
Tucson, AZ 85721
(602) 326-6410

Central Arkansas Peace Corps Association
5907 C Street
Little Rock, AR 72205
(501) 663-6207

Peace Corps Alumni of Los Angeles
P.O. Box 24767
Los Angeles, CA 90024
(818) 570-9235

Eastern California RPCVs
P.O. Box 1717
Mammoth Lakes, CA 93456

Sacramento Valley RPCVs
P.O. Box 161163
Sacramento, CA 95816
(916) 763-0845

San Diego Peace Corps Association
P.O. Box 26565
San Diego, CA 92196
(619) 276-7871

NORCAL Peace Corps Association
P.O. Box 2547
San Francisco, CA 94126
(415) 933-4490

Peace Corps Alumni of Colorado
Box 18995
Denver, CO 80218
(303) 442-3742

Connecticut RPCVs
P.O. Box 8614
New Haven, CT 06531
(203) 397-1849

RPCV/Washington
P.O. Box 66101
Washington, DC 20035-6101
(202) 544-5063

RPCVs of South Florida, Inc.
2050 Coral Way, Suite 602
Miami, FL 33145
(305) 868-8344

Central Florida RPCVs
1333 Utah Boulevard
Orlando, FL 32803

**North Florida Peace Corps
Association**
1500 Belleau Wood
Tallahassee, FL 32312
(904) 386-8672

Atlanta Area RPCVs
P.O. Box 687
Decatur, GA 30031-0687
(404) 934-7597

Hawaii RPCV Association
P.O. Box 402
Honolulu, HI 96809
(808) 526-0110

Idaho RPCVs
2648 Gourley Street
Boise, ID 83705-4026
(208) 344-6110

Chicago Area RPCVs
Box 1149
Chicago, IL 60690
(312) 878-9477

Indiana RPCVs
P.O. Box 2627
Indianapolis, IN 46202
(317) 926-0665

Iowa Peace Corps Association
3800 Crestmoor Place
Des Moines, IA 50310-4327
(515) 278-6048

Kansas RPCVs
636 North Lakeside Drive
Andover, KS 67002
(316) 773-0782

Kentucky RPCVs
2206 Merrick Road
Louisville, KY 40207

Louisiana RPCVs
6008 Catina Street
New Orleans, LA 70124
(504) 488-2698

Maine RPCVs
P.O. Box 8032
Portland, ME 04104
(207) 873-3761

Maryland Returned Volunteers
300 East University Parkway
Baltimore, MD 21218
(410) 235-4197

Boston Area RPCVs
P.O. Box 35364
Brighton, MA 02135
(617) 926-7814

Southeastern Michigan RPCVs
P.O. Box 725075
Berkley, MI 48072
(313) 663-5032

RPCVs of West Michigan
859 Nevada Street SE
Grand Rapids, MI 49507
(616) 245-6793

Minnesota RPCVs
P.O. Box 6413
Minneapolis, MN 55406
(612) 798-5748

Northeast Mississippi RPCVs
P.O. Box 9690
MSU, MS 39762
(601) 323-8768

Missouri RPCVs
Box 16
Amsterdam, MO 64730

Western Montana RPCVs
1729 North Avenue West
Missoula, MT 59801
(406) 586-4266

Nebraska Area RPCVs
905 Mercer Boulevard
Omaha, NE 68131
(402) 551-3459

Southern Nevada RPCVs
2987 Palma Vista Circle
Las Vegas, NV 89109
(702) 734-1407

RPCVs of New Jersey
14 Glenwood Avenue
Jersey City, NJ 07306
(201) 434-3888

New Mexico Peace Corps Association
Box 1971
Santa Fe, NM 87504
(505) 983-7342

RPCVs of Greater New York
P.O. Box 3336
New York, NY 10017-9998

North Carolina Peace Corps Association
615 Willard Place
Raleigh, NC 27603
(919) 286-6045

North Dakota Peace Corps Association
1117 3rd Avenue South
Fargo, ND 58103
(701) 293-3577

Central Ohio Returned Volunteers
2120 Fyffe Road, Room 113
Agriculture Administration Building
Columbus, OH 43210-1099
(614) 844-5906

Toledo RPCVs
P.O. Box 72
Toledo, OH 43697

Oklahoma RPCVs
716 South Willis
Stillwater, OK 74074
(405) 377-1653

RPCVs of Oregon, Portland
P.O. Box 802
Portland, OR 97207
(503) 236-5838

Philadelphia Area Peace Corps Association
P.O. Box 42542
Philadelphia, PA 19101

Puerto Rico RPCVs
P.O. Box 595
Juana Diaz, PR 00665-0595
(809) 837-3587

Rhode Island RPCVs
62 Rodman Street
Narragansett, RI 02882
(401) 783-4235

RPCVs of South Carolina
1127 Blake Drive
Cayce, SC 29169
(803) 769-2358

Tennessee RPCVs
1359 Linden Avenue, #4
Memphis, TN 38104
(901) 274-9438

Dallas Fort Worth RPCVs
P.O. Box 595832
Dallas, TX 75359-5832
(214) 357-8337

Gulf Coast Council of RPCVs
1000 Campbell Road, Suite 208-687
Houston, TX 77055
(713) 960-1540

Utah RPCVs
c/o 1790 Bonanza Drive, Suite 230
P.O. Box 2730
Park City, UT 84060

Green Mountain RPCVs
RR 1, Box 1570
Plainfield, VT 05667
(802) 254-8654

Returned Action Volunteers of NW
PC Recruiting Office
2001 6th Avenue, #1776
Seattle, WA 98121

RPCVs of West Virginia
1819 Huber Road
Charleston, WV 25314-2231

RPCVs of Wisconsin, Madison
P.O. Box 1012
Madison, WI 53701
(608) 257-2271

RPCVs of Wisconsin, Milwaukee
P.O. Box 1193
Milwaukee, WI 53201-1193
(414) 271-3658

Peace Corps Information Online

www.peacecorps.gov
Peace Corps' official website. Includes program-specific information, "how to apply" section, frequently asked questions, returned volunteer section, contact information, diversity discussion, and more.

www.concentric.net/~jmuehl/ pcinfon.shtml
The Peace Corps Information Network. Self-described as "a website dedicated to helping prospective Peace Corps volunteers find each other and find returned (or current) Peace Corps volunteers to answer any questions they may have." Includes an extensive RPCV database, an active bulletin board, and numerous Peace Corps–related links, including several of those listed here.

www.rpcv.org
National Peace Corps Association (NPCA) website. Aimed at the RPCV community, but provides links to other PC-related organizations, e-mail address search capabilities (to find RPCVs from specific countries), and more.

www.umeais.maine.edu/~career/ pc/PCORPS.HTML
Peace Corps website at the University of Maine. Provides straightforward information on Peace Corps' benefits and challenges. Also has program, training, and geographic information.

www.crpca.org
The Columbia River Peace Corps Association website. Includes a section for prospective volunteers entitled "What Should I Bring?" Also provides links for RPCVs.

www.welcome.to/PCV-L
The "Peace Corps Story Teller" website. Includes letters and pictures from Peace Corps volunteers, and a Peace Corps Site-of-the-Month link.

www.royalpages.com/family
Peace Corps Family Support Group website. Provides information for family members of PCVs, including care package tips, advice for visiting PCVs, country-specific information, overseas PC offices and contact information, and a bulletin board/chat room for contacting other families of PCVs.

www.geocities.com/~lgbrpcv
Lesbian/Gay/Bisexual RPCV home page. Includes volunteer stories, information and discussions on gay issues for applicants, Peace Corps and human rights links, and more.

www.ets.uidaho.edu/winr/ parker_2.htm
Article entitled "Combining Peace Corps Service with a Master's Degree," describing the Master's International Program. Part of the University of Idaho's Women In Natural Resources newsletter.

www.s_t.com/daily/11-96/ 11-03-96/f07bu161.htm
Article by Karen Mills (Associated Press writer) entitled "Peace Corps looks for new crop of experienced, older volunteers."

About the Author

DILLON BANERJEE served as an agroforestry volunteer in the Peace Corps from 1994 to 1996 in Belo, Cameroon. He has also spent three years in the Philippines and two years in Indonesia. He received a B.A. from the College of William and Mary in Williamsburg, Virginia, where he studied political science and international economics. He earned an M.A. in International Development from the School of International Service (SIS) at the American University in Washington, DC. Having worked at the U.S. Environmental Protection Agency for the past three years, Dillon most recently accepted a foreign service officer position with the U.S. Agency for International Development and looks forward to returning overseas with his wife, Sarah, in the near future.

Index

V

Vacation days, 106, 116, 122
Vegetarian volunteers, 52–53
Visits. *See also* Travel
    back to the States, 116
    by friends and family, 106–7
Volunteer leaders (PCVLs), 99, 114
Volunteers (PCVs).
        See also Returned volunteers
    dating, 94–95
    female, 74–75
    gay and lesbian, 11
    harassment of, 73–75
    local acceptance of, 55–56
    married, 7
    minority, 12, 138
    number of, 138
    over fifty, 9–10, 138
    seeing/visiting other, 88–91
    in serious relationships, 8
    statistics about, 138
    stereotypes of, 55–56, 103
    vegetarian, 52–53

W

Water
    purification, 27
    running, 46–48
Websites, 173
Weight loss/gain, 64–65
Women
    pregnancy, 69–70
    sexual harassment, 74–75
Work schedule, 98
Worms, 62–63

Y

Youth development, 142, 147